From Beneath the Ice

A tale of struggle and triumph from PTSD and mental illness

For my amazing wife and my beautiful children.
Without all of you, I would not be here, living the best of my days.
I am forever grateful.

Copyright © 2024 by Todd Arkyn Crush

All Rights Reserved

Editor: Lesli Crush

Cover design by John Silva

Back cover image: Caitlin Beasley

ISBN: 9798879622324

Table of Contents

　　Prologue

1. Nearly the End
2. Childhood
3. The First Notes
4. Within Her Light
5. Unraveling
6. Parenthood
7. One Way Ticket
8. Heavy Days
9. The Curse
10. Crisis
11. Duality
12. Breaking Away
13. An Unexpected Story
14. After the Storm
15. Departure
16. Fortitude
17. Shelter
18. Leaving Home, Again
19. Down
20. A New Face
21. Among the Horses
22. The Scorpion
23. Visitations
24. A Chance of Clouds
25. Upon These Wings
26. End of the Line
27. Out There Again
28. The Manic Cabin
29. In the Midst of Things
30. Searching
31. Beginning to Believe
32. I Am....
33. Love
34. Pandemic
35. Transformation
36. One Step Forward, Two Steps...
37. And Still, the Past
38. Embracing Change
39. Up On the Stage
40. Pushing Through
41. Power Run
42. Above It All

PROLOGUE

If your life was a book, would you read it? Would it be a harrowing adventure, a desolate tragedy, or a love story? This book is all those things. It is a gripping story about my life and struggles with childhood abuse and mental illness. It chronicles how I coped with trauma and schizophrenia. I am not an expert or a professional. I am a survivor. Living in the wilderness is dangerous, even life-threatening. It was the path I chose, but it came with great sacrifice. Certainly, there were safer routes that would have lessened the heartache my family endured.

I never intentionally set out to hurt anyone, especially my children and my first wife. Through my struggles, I certainly did. Fear ruled me and because of my torment, I failed to trust them. I deeply regret this. I hope through writing this, they will find solace in why I took this path and can grant me forgiveness.

What could have been a better path? I know if I had read a book like this 25 years ago, I would have had hope. I would have opened up to my wife about my struggles. I would have sought help. Although it's not a perfect system, professional help and medication are better choices. Getting the right combination took me years of trial and error. NEVER SETTLE. If your doctor isn't listening, get another doctor. Medications stop working and have side effects. the idea is to have the best quality of life with the least symptoms. It's a balance, but a big reason why I am sitting here today.

My main purpose in writing this book is to help people. There needs to be more dialogue about mental illness. It has definitely improved since my schizophrenia hit 25 years ago, but we are still in the dark ages. Help is out there, and I am doing my best to foster conversation, awareness, and end the stigma. Together, each one of us has a choice. We can choose to show compassion instead of fear. We can listen instead of walking away. We can seek to understand instead of judging.

When I began this journey to chronicle my life, I knew I had to be courageous if I wanted to help others. Sharing with true authenticity and raw vulnerability has been challenging, even triggering at times. But it's working. In the few short months before publication, thousands of people have reached out to me about this book. It has already touched so many lives.

I was contacted by a mother of a teenage son who was exhibiting early signs of schizophrenia. He was closed off from the world and was almost completely nonverbal. She wanted to know what he was experiencing. I shared, she shared, and together we helped. He is now talking more about what is happening to him, and they are having conversations about treatment and healing.

Schizophrenia can be slippery. You're dealing with alternate versions of reality after all. We all might see blue, but exactly what shade? There's no way to tell. A woman reached out to me about her mother-in-law. She is hearing the neighbors' voices inside her own home. She is convinced they are watching her and keeps searching for hidden cameras. I conveyed my own turmoil, about checking every outlet, switch, and light bulb in my apartment over and over again. For weeks, I had a steady supply of light bulbs and outlet covers piled up in the center of the living room. I still felt that someone was listening. Now, I am the one listening. Since I talked with her, they were able to convince her mother-in-law to go to the hospital for evaluation.

I have known many people with mental illness who didn't survive. My friend, Janice, was an artist. I was working with her to design covers for my albums. Her depression was so dark, that it slowly stole her away. I met with her one day and the next, she was gone.

I hope that those who have survived may read this book and see my scars as a map to help them navigate a new direction of possibility. Instead of seeing broken pieces, may they see hope. May they use this map in their darkest moments as a guide to illuminate their own path through. The true accomplishment of this book will be not in its ability to show my struggle and triumph with mental illness, but to witness that triumph in others.

Be strong warriors,

Todd Arkyn Crush

TRIGGER WARNING: This book contains descriptions of suicidal ideation, near-death experiences, abuse, and schizophrenic hallucinations and symptoms. Please proceed with caution.

WARNING: The following text features activities performed either by professionals or under the advice of professionals. Accordingly, the author and his staff and publishers must insist that no one attempts to re-create or re-enact any activity described or outlined within this treatise.

1

NEARLY THE END

*I am not what happened to me,
I am what I choose to become.*

Carl Jung

In my darkest moment, as the light slowly faded in my mind, I could hear the distant echo of my children's laughter. As life seemed to be slipping away, the sound of their smiles was a beacon to my instinct to survive. I forced myself to crawl from the bed. My body was shutting down. It was as if I was moving through concrete as I summoned my last breath of hope. I pushed through, but consciousness escaped me. The thought of my kids was a piercing dream and I slowly came to....

Holding my phone like a prayer.

I dialed 911.

Everything in me wanted the voice to stop, to let the sleeping pills I had taken run their course. At the same time, everything in me wanted to live, to see my kids another day. Drake, with his dark, sinister voice, was yelling at me.

'PUT DOWN THE PHONE YOU LOSER! NOBODY WILL CARE THAT YOU ARE GONE. YOU NEVER AMOUNTED TO ANYTHING. YOU'RE WORTHLESS. DIE! DIE! DIE! DIE! DIE!'

I was at a point I had never been in my whole life. I just wanted it to stop and was prepared to die in order for that to happen. I had been enduring his cruel, demeaning voice for 12 hours. I slammed my fist into the side of my head several times. It was the only way I could think of to try to silence him. His voice was chewing away vigorously at my soul. It didn't work, but it jolted me awake long enough to let living win. With the overdose of sleeping pills kicking in, my children's laughter pulled me out of the darkness. Alongside them in that moment, I chose life.

The voices and hallucinations had ravaged me for seven years prior to this suicide attempt. From one moment to the next, I never knew if what I was experiencing was reality. At any time, I could hear or see something that wasn't really there. From the moment my first hallucination appeared, I was terrified that I would be locked in an institution forever. In this constant state of fear, I felt trapped to endure all of this completely on my own.

This meant sitting still and watching a movie with my family while Fred was throwing knives at the wall. It meant resisting the urge to check the house for intruders that I could hear in the other room. There were no private, personal moments without the fear of being invaded by hallucinations.

I had three little kids, a wife, and a successful career. Schizophrenia destroyed all of that. I couldn't function in any capacity. I couldn't work, couldn't enjoy my kids, couldn't even go to the grocery store without fear and absolute panic. I couldn't. It's difficult going through everyday life never knowing when your mind is going to be hijacked. Reality is no longer lucid, so you are always on edge.

Take a moment to look up from this page, and witness everything around you. Notice the sounds of the day, the music playing, the feel of your clothes against your skin, or the things you see outside the window. Now, imagine not being able to tell *if any of that is real.* This is schizophrenia. At any given moment, you are constantly questioning what is happening around you. At any given moment someone could shout at you from the other room, or you could turn to see someone you don't know...standing in your kitchen holding a knife.

Perhaps I'm getting a little ahead of myself. Let's go back to the beginning.

2

CHILDHOOD

Hardships often prepare ordinary people for an extraordinary destiny.

C. S. Lewis

Alone in the dark, crying out, an infant boy lay waiting, for anyone. Fragile and new to life, everything in him screamed out to be held, to be loved. Shivering and frightened, his cries echoed throughout the large cathedral.

Old St. Mary's Catholic church in downtown Milwaukee Wisconsin was cold, frozen with November's breath. The church, built in the mid-19th century, was closed for renovations. Temperatures were in the low 30s and the heat was off. Scared, hungry, and wrapped only in a thin blanket, the tiny baby waited. Father John had forgotten his sermon papers that day, so he stopped by to pick them up. As he entered the chapel, he heard the newborn's cries. The baby was me.

No one knows how long I was there, where I had come from, or why I was abandoned. Sadly, although I didn't know it at the time, this fear of being alone and isolated in the dark would become a recurring theme in my life for years to come.

Many years later, I met the priest who found me. He was old but remembered the incident very well. It was still shocking to him, and he recalled driving me to the hospital. "At first, I couldn't believe what I was hearing. I thought maybe someone had left a radio on. It took me a while to find you, you were all the way at the back. I have thought often about holding you that day, wondering where your path had taken you." His eyes held my gaze with a depth and compassion that radiated through me like the first warm day of spring. "I didn't have far to go, but every minute of that drive my heart was racing and aching for you. You were quiet on the way to the hospital, almost as if you knew that now, you would be okay."

Because I was left at the church, I don't know the actual day of my birth. I was adopted by a married couple as an infant shortly after I was found. For many years, I thought they were my birth parents. The facts surrounding my birth were never discussed when I was young. I still don't know who my biological parents are or why they left me. Despite my ever-present paranoia at the time, about five years ago, I decided to take a DNA test to find out more about my heritage. To my surprise, I discovered I am 84% Norwegian. I was told that most likely both my parents and grandparents were natives of Norway. At the time, I thought... maybe my parents were immigrants and too scared to take me to a hospital; maybe my mother was young, afraid, and alone. I may never know the full story, but finding out where I came from gave me a sense of belonging that I had never had.

Life was not very good with my adoptive parents. My dad was a busy attorney. He worked long hours and traveled often. My mother was an elementary school teacher and was always home. She was ruthless in her criticism and antagonism of me. I could never seem to do anything right and was made to feel like a burden. She constantly berated me and made a point to emphasize how worthless or pathetic I was. Seemingly at every turn, she was against me. Her words cut deeper than any knife ever could, and even now they still pervade my mind.

Every time someone corrects me, I attempt something new, or do much of anything at all (including writing this book), the critical voice of my mother is in my head. For a long time, the self-doubt was crippling, and the soundtrack to my life was completely negative. To this day, verbal abuse remains the worst memory of my childhood. Hearing things like, "You'll never amount to anything!" or "You're always in the way!" still echo through my thoughts and invade my dreams.

A very close second to the torment of persistent insults was 'The Closet'. I lived in a big house with many rooms. There was a small closet near the front hall. It was tucked away from the rest of the house, so no one passed by there on most occasions. It was in this closet where my mother would take me and lock me away in the dark. Frequently, this happened for multiple days at a time. I dreaded the weekends. The closet was a living hell that only compounded how terrible I felt about myself.

The impending dread of being locked away, alone in the dark, haunted me constantly. In those endless hours, the permeating eerie silence would suddenly be broken. The disparaging voice of my mother would abruptly ring out "Do you think the world revolves around you?" "Everything about you is just so wrong..." Even in her absence, her words fell like hammers there in the dark.

As the Archaic Greek poet, Sappho said: "What cannot be said, will be wept." I feel that saying in my bones. I cried an ocean of tears in that desolate place. In my young mind, I would try to find a reason why I was locked away. When I was put in the closet because of an emotional outburst, I could at least look at what happened and say, 'Well that's why...' There were other times though, when I would be playing with the dog or watching TV quietly, and I was ushered off to the closet with no explanation. Those were the hardest. I sat there in the dark wondering what I had done wrong. Even more so, contemplating if something was truly wrong with me. I was broken. I spent most of my childhood in absolute despair. I didn't feel loved, heard, seen, or wanted. Even now, over 40 years later, I am tormented by the feeling that I have done or soon will do something wrong and be caged in there all over again. When I see a closet door left ajar, I think of those long dark nights alone, crying myself to sleep on that cold, relentless floor.

As far as I know, my brother never knew about me being in the closet. He was also adopted. He is four years younger than me, so he was much too little to do anything or even understand what was happening. I am uncertain if my dad knew. I want to believe that he did not. Part of me feels that he didn't know, and another part feels that he did. I have wondered if he knew, maybe that was the reason he seemed to overcompensate by taking me to do fun things, such as going to Chicago Cubs games. I almost asked him several times, but in the end, I let it go. There are days now that I wish I had asked him. My mind is unsettled often, pondering what might have been.

The haunting memories of my mother's verbal and mental abuse affect my daily life when I think about going out in public. I spend almost every second wondering what everybody is thinking about me. From a very early age, this was ingrained into my fragile mind. My parents were extremely concerned about their positions in the community. I was constantly berated for just being a kid and for doing things normal kids do. I would hear things like "What is everyone going to think about us? You are a dark mark upon this family. Why can't you be more like xxx?"

A large portion of this angst came from the fact that I was not like other kids. I was extremely intelligent, and eccentric in my behaviors. In hindsight, I was most likely bored. The criticism taught me that something was inherently wrong with me. I was led to believe that whatever I was made of, was wrong. From a very young age, I was 'leveled up' in school. On the second day of kindergarten, I was found reading Carl Sagan on the playground, so I was moved to first grade. From there, I quickly ascended through, skipping third and part of fifth grade. For the rest of my schooling, all the way through college, I was much younger than everyone else. I didn't seem to fit in anywhere. I couldn't relate to any of the other kids at school. I had nobody to confide in or even distract myself with most of the time. I don't say any of this egotistically, only to make a point. All the kids I knew, and a good portion of the adults, were boring to talk to. This started very early in my life.

It didn't help that my mother kept me from having a normal social life. I wasn't allowed to have friends over to the house and was very rarely allowed to go to anyone else's home. It was bad enough that the kids saw me as a know-it-all, but the lack of interaction set in stone the fact that I was different. Perhaps she didn't want me to see how other kids were living. She was most likely worried I might tell someone how I was being treated. The isolation was hard, and it made me feel that much more broken.

Our family was very stoic and unemotional. No one discussed feelings or showed emotions about anything. If I was struggling, I was expected to go somewhere and get through it on my own. From the very beginning, I was a very lively kid when it came to emotions. I had to let them out and I most certainly did. This caused great discord within the family. When something was bothering me, I would speak up and keep at it until I felt better. This often got me into trouble. My punishment was always severe.

On the other side of my childhood, there was music. Music was my lifeboat, my anchor in the dark. When I was four years old, a family friend took me to the record store. His name was Mike. I had a record player and had been listening to the university jazz program on my radio at night. Imagine walking into your favorite candy store as a little kid and your grandma telling you to pick out your favorite candy bar or dessert. This was the music store for me. I had already chosen the album I wanted - Bill Evans, Sunday at the Village Vanguard. There was a look of amazement and delight when I told the music store employee what I was looking for. He was surprised that someone so young was selecting such an iconic album. A few weeks later, I returned and requested John Coltrane's Olé. He was equally amused. I will never forget bringing that first album home, smelling the newness of the vinyl, and putting it on. We had a piano, and by that afternoon, I had moved the record player into the piano room and was trying to play along to my new favorite possession.

Another outlet for me as a child was baseball. Frequently, my father would take me to Cubs games at Wrigley Field. I remember the first time we went. It was mid-summer, I was five, and the Ivy was full and lush along the outfield wall. I took in the incredible beauty of it all. Until that time, I had only seen these images on television. The immaculate field, interrupted graciously by dirt and white chalk; the organ and the announcer, keeping pace with the only thing that mattered to me for those few hours. I remember around the second inning, and I have no idea why, but a fight broke out on the field. Suddenly all the players were crashing together in a medieval kind of mele. I was in shock. My heart was racing, and I remember my young mind thinking, what if the fight comes up here?

It was over quickly, and the game resumed. I don't know who won that day, but I was a Cubs fan for life. I still watch almost every game, and when they won the World Series in 2016, it meant a great deal to me. I remember sitting in my apartment all alone, soaking up the glow of the television and reveling in the victory. Besides baseball and music, however, there was not a great deal of joy in my young life.

Music was a refuge for me, even when I was locked away. I had made a number of white and black strips of paper that I would carry around with me in my pocket. When I was put in the closet, I would sit in there with my paper piano, singing the notes as I played them so very softly. In my mind, I was in a great concert hall, free of the reigns of torment from my mother.

As horrible as the closet was, in the dark with no bathroom, my mind racing and full of intrusive thoughts; part of me enjoyed the break from the verbal abuse that was constantly spilling out of my mother. At least in the closet, I didn't have to hear it out loud. That's not to say the audio tape of her voice didn't play on endlessly in my head, as it still does from time to time, but it was better. It was hell, but it was a quiet hell.

As I grew older, the feeling of not being loved or wanted was carried heavily into my adult relationships, especially with women. Two main themes prevailed. First, I felt afraid of letting anyone see the real me because I had been taught for my entire life that the real me was ugly and terrible. I kept everyone at a distance. Second, I felt unlovable. I was quick to keep my heart hidden, for fear of rejection or abandonment. These dark feelings of separation led me to become as such – unlovable.

Another problem in relationships, not just romantic involvement, but with friends and colleagues, pervaded because I was constantly on edge, thinking I would do something horribly wrong. I analyzed every word, but at the same time would get caught up talking away. Afterward, I would spend endless nights overthinking how they must be feeling about what I had said; or more accurately, had said wrong.

As a child, relationships of any kind were exceptionally difficult. I considered the fact that maybe I should play dumb and just fit in with all the other kids. Maybe then I would shine in my mother's eyes. Maybe then I would be what she wanted. I knew that I couldn't though. That seal had already been broken in kindergarten when they made me skip a grade. The cat was out of the bag. I couldn't go back, but how could I keep going?

I seemed to be met by sheer disappointment at every turn. Nothing was ever good enough. Nothing was ever right. Nothing seemed to satisfy my mother's sour heart. I sat in that dark closet, for endless hours, as days turned into nights, contemplating a solution to that enigma. One never came.

3

THE FIRST NOTES

Music is the soul out loud.

Todd Arkyn Crush

Music spoke to me. I discovered that every time I played along to that Bill Evans record, I heard something new. The shape of a chord, an accent note, or a shift in the rhythm all came through over and over to me. Amid all the torment in my life at that time, music quickly became a formidable place I could go and be safe. It was a shelter where I felt far away from all that was threatening or scaring me. I still go there to this day.

I have made a lifetime of using music to escape the crazy hallucinations and thoughts that plague my everyday life. Schizophrenia, along with any mental illness or trauma, is extremely difficult, sometimes unbearable. Music makes it survivable. Music has been a lifeline to me on countless occasions. It has literally saved my life. My hallucinations have brought me to the brink of suicide several times, and music has been there to pull me back.

A notable example of this was when I was living in Arkansas in a tiny mountain town after my backpacking trip. I was isolated and had no way to get help or meds. I was hallucinating daily, and my thoughts quickly declined into desperation. The thoughts of ending it all began to haunt me. I immersed myself in the music of Brad Mehldau. I put it on as loud as it would go and attempted to play along with my bass.

I got lost in it.

Deep inside the complex harmonies and rhythms, my soul sought respite from what plagued my mind. For a few hours, I was free. After each session, I was no longer suicidal. I had the will to play again the next day, and then the next. It gave me a solace that is hard to put into words. Maybe that's why I've always favored instrumental, improvised music. The expression of the soul without words, a melody of the spirit; changing lives with every note.

This suicidal pattern has repeated itself over and over again in my life. I have been near the end so many times, but during every visit to that dark and desolate place, there was music. When my world would spiral into blackness, music was there to bring me back to life.

Music helped me write this book. The agonizing parts about my childhood and mental illness were hard. It was like reliving the horrors as I wrote them down. I needed music all over again. There were days that I could only write for ten minutes, and then I would play my bass for an hour, to reset myself so I could write again. It was arduous, but in the end, the most therapeutic experience of my entire life.

I know now that I have a gift for music, its language and feel, but back then it was a beam of light in a dark room; guiding me home every time. In my childhood, music was my sanctuary. It built itself amidst the ruins that were my broken self-image. After a little while, I got pretty good at playing along with the Bill Evans record. I bought more. At four years old, I had no idea what notes I was playing, I just memorized what sounded good and kept all those notes in my head.

All of this seemed to intensify the abuse at home. It was as if my mother felt threatened by me and needed to keep me down. She was also a piano player, so maybe she was intimidated by my proficiency at such a young age with no instruction whatsoever. Thankfully, she never took away the piano. Sure, I was in a closet a lot, but I practiced in there too. When I got out, my records and piano were waiting for me every single time.

As time went on, my time in the closet increased. The unrelenting, demeaning, and critical banter continued. The better I did in school, or anything else for that matter, the worse it got. But I kept pushing. Maybe, just maybe I thought.... the next thing I do will change her mind. I didn't feel very good about myself. I believed I was broken. I had no friends. Everyone in my classes was three years older than me and didn't know what to make of me.

When I was a freshman in high school, my parents sat me down and told me I was adopted. I was shocked and angry that they had waited so long to tell me. I was also a little relieved. The relief came because I was grateful to be unrelated to them. It made my feelings about the way they had treated me more easily validated. Everything suddenly made more sense. They told me my biological parents were older and just didn't want any more kids, which was a total lie. I understand it would have been hard to tell me I had been left at a church as an infant. That is kind of a harsh truth to tell a young mind. Would it have been any worse than what they were putting me through every day? NO.

Around this time, I started to struggle more with not being able to voice my emotions constructively. I had been shut off from having feelings for so long that when I finally tried to communicate, it escalated to yelling and screaming regularly, so I was sent to therapy. The therapy helped; I was allowed to vent my frustrations about my mother without fear of repercussions. After every single session, she would grill me about what I talked about. I would make something up. I would tell her I was talking about this girl at school or whatever. It didn't dawn on me until many years later that she was probably trying to find out if I was telling the therapist about being locked in the closet along with the verbal and emotional abuse. I never did. I often wonder now what would have happened if I had. I don't know why I never told the therapist. I probably thought I would just be in even more trouble. Part of me knows that my mother would have denied everything. Much as she is guaranteed to do with the publication of this book.

I look back now and examine everything that was going on in my life and know that my emotional eruptions were completely understandable. Even so, because of my outbursts, I was put on medication. I don't remember what kind, just that it made my mouth really dry, and I didn't feel quite like myself. I felt flat emotionally. Things I used to get excited about were now more of an 'oh well'. Even music didn't delight me the way that it used to. I still played, but it didn't bring me the same joy.

One of the worst things about being prescribed this drug was that now more than ever, it seemed like I was not allowed to have feelings of any kind. Even the slightest expression of emotion was met sternly with "Did you take your medication?" It made me feel even more broken. I couldn't seem to do anything right. I was screaming inside every moment but remained mute. I didn't understand why everyone else was allowed to have outbursts and emotions, but I was not. It taught me, in my developing years, to stay hidden. To deal with everything quietly and on my own. It taught me that I was damaged, and more than ever that I would always be alone.

In those formative years, I learned that while everyone else's articulations of feeling were okay, mine were not. I learned that a large part of what made me human was unacceptable.

4

WITHIN HER LIGHT

*The world is full of magic things,
patiently waiting for our senses to grow sharper.*

W.B. Yeats.

One of the people who made the most indelible impact on my life was my grandmother. She lived on an old chicken farm about an hour away, and I remember the joy of riding there in the car. Those roads led to heaven, and the lines on her face became the roads I knew by heart.

She was reverently kind, wise, and taught me so much about the world. On a weekend here and there, she was the glimpse of a childhood I could have only dreamed of. I wanted so much to tell her what was happening at home. About how her daughter was treating me, but I was afraid if I said anything I would never see her again. No more riding on the tractor, playing with the dog, dancing to records, or hearing stories about the old days.

When I was seven, she seemed to sense that I was searching for something bigger. I remember the sun coming in through the windows in the kitchen, lighting up the cabinets with vignettes of the big walnut trees in the yard. We sat down and she presented a few books about Buddhism. I took to it immediately and read all I could about it. Meditation became another haven, that I could do anywhere, at any time. I memorized Buddhist philosophies, stories, and ideals. The exposure to these ideas created a foundation of strength in me at a very early age. I appeared broken and meek on the outside, but deep down it was something to stand on. I stood there alone, but I stood, nonetheless.

When I was 13, after six years of studying Buddhism, I reached out and was accepted to study at a temple in India. Never in my wildest dreams did I imagine that my parents would let me go, especially my mother. She had, after all, kept me from going to friends' houses for my entire childhood. But, to my complete amazement, they said yes. Maybe the thought of not having me around for three months was very appealing to them. I didn't really care. I was elated to be going, not just to study, but primarily to get as far away from them as I possibly could.

I remember the long flight, and landing in a strange place in the middle of the night. I managed to get a cab and realized quickly that I was in for the craziest ride of my life. The driver, and everyone else, paid no attention to any traffic laws whatsoever. It was absolute chaos at the highest speeds possible. By the time we left the city, my nerves were completely frayed, and I was grateful to be on a lonely stretch of road. We were still going fast, but at least all the other cars were gone.

The temple was in a valley, flanked on every side by steep hills. It looked like it had been there for a thousand years. I was greeted by two monks, who looked exactly like you would expect them to look, bald, with robes and sandals. They said nothing, just a slight bow of their heads, and they led me to a small room that was to be mine for the duration of my stay. In it was a cot, a lamp, and a small table with a ceramic bowl. That was it.

My days there were largely filled with meditation. It was terribly hot with a million flies buzzing around, so meditation in this place was much more difficult than in my air-conditioned room back home. A monk was walking around with a bamboo stick. His job was to whack you on the back if you fell asleep. I never did. It was impossible with all the flies, but it was a reminder to stay focused, nonetheless.

We did menial tasks, like cleaning a giant rug by hand and washing and preparing the rice. Life there was simple and deliberate. I was ill-prepared for the flood of thoughts and emotions that came washing over me during meditation. As Robert Pirsig said, "The only Zen you'll find on the tops of mountains is the Zen you bring up there." This is very true, but it goes both ways. You bring everything else up there with you too. Sitting in meditation is very difficult because your mind turns on like a waterfall; cascading down on you with every thought and feeling you've ever had all at once. For quite some time, my mother's voice was there for every single meditation and every night alone in that tiny room. I had traveled halfway around the world, to realize that the closet wasn't at home, it was in my head.

Towards the end, I was starting to have more positive meditation experiences. I remember waiting and waiting to see the head monk and worrying that I was going to have to leave before I met with him. I tried not to ask too often, but I was told every time "Not ready." It didn't take me long to realize it was me they were referring to when saying those words, not the head monk.

The day finally did come about a week before my departure. I had never been in that room of the temple before. It was modest and functional. I sat on a cushion across from him and we just looked at each other for what seemed like forever. His gaze was comforting and unsettling at the same time. I felt as if he knew everything I was thinking, and that no matter what I said, it would be the wrong thing.

Finally, he asked, "Who are you?" I told him my name. "No, who *are* you?" I paused. My brain was racing a thousand miles an hour trying to come up with something wise to say. "I am helpful." This seemed to please him, and he nodded. "Who are you without words?" Everything in my mind came to a screeching halt. For the first moment in my life, I had complete clarity. No intrusive thoughts or worries, no mother, no past, no closet, no self. I just sat there clear as a glass of water.

I recognized the significance of what I was experiencing and also realized that I needed to answer his question, "Who are you without words?" There was a small vase of flowers next to us and I observed that the flowers were giving their beauty and fragrance to us while asking nothing in return. I thought this was a good metaphor for how to approach life. I pulled a flower from the vase and offered it to him in silence. He smiled and let out a joyful big-belly laugh. He gestured for me to stand and then gave me a very long and sincere hug. After that, he sat back down and smiled. He gave the slightest bow of his head and I knew that my time was up.

I don't remember much about the rest of that trip, but I do know that the foundation I had started with music grew even stronger from my experience at the temple. I still study Buddhism and meditate from time to time. I like to think of my daily run as a form of moving meditation. I stand firmly upon those same roots even now, knowing that no matter what happens, I will be alright.

5

UNRAVELING

*The drops of rain make a hole in the stone,
not by violence, but by oft falling.*

Lucretius

My primary socialization was devoid of affection and connection. As a family, we didn't hug. We didn't say I love you. We didn't talk about our feelings. If there was an argument or something major happened, we all went to our rooms and started the next day as if nothing ever happened. That always bothered me, and it affects me to this day. I am an emotional person. I need to express myself. As a child, those aspects of me were suppressed and I was left to suffer through my thoughts and feelings alone in the darkness – whether I was in the dreadful closet or in my head.

Even to this day, when feelings arise, I am inclined to bury them deeply. Without a positive outlet or a safe place to share, I tend to lash out at small things for no apparent reason. I know this type of behavior is upsetting to everyone involved. It troubles me greatly and it used to be extremely confusing because I had yet to understand why I was reacting this way.

Only recently, with the help of my amazing wife and a good therapist, have I begun the process of unwinding the trauma responses and been better able to rationalize my reactions. Learning to understand how I am feeling takes patience and practice. The more I am consciously aware of my emotions, the better able I am to express them in a healthy way. Having a supportive partner who encourages my growth has been so helpful. We stay committed to communication on all levels.

When problems arise, disappearing and later acting as if nothing happened, doesn't resolve anything. You cease to grow. This was an important lesson for me to learn. Talking through what happened, how it made you feel, and listening to others facilitates a medium in which everyone benefits and grows individually, and as a family. I have discovered this recently in my adult life. My wife, daughter, and bonus daughter have really helped expand my emotional intelligence by talking through my outbursts. They have helped me slowly remove the negative soundtrack in my head, and replace it with an increasingly positive one. I know that I have done a lot of the work myself, but without their loving support and encouragement, I would not have made the same progress.

From a very early age, I was determined not to repeat the patterns of behavior I had been shown as a child. For a long time as an adult, I was failing at this. I certainly didn't lock anyone in a closet or verbally abuse them, but when things got tough, I hid. In the wilderness, in music, or inside myself. I practiced a fair amount of avoidance behavior with my own children, running endlessly and working long hours. It was only within the last few years that I realized; that by living this way, I was still in the closet.

When I was 25, I was married, with two young children. One day, my wife and kids were gone, and I was home alone. I was refinishing a buffet table in the dining room in front of a window. I looked out, and saw a girl, about 12 years old, facing the window and talking at me from the driveway. I went out to see if she needed help. When I stepped outside, she was gone. I looked all over our yard for her. Eventually, I gave up and came back inside. She was standing in our dining room. She was still talking, but there was no sound. I asked her if I could help. I asked her what her name was. I asked her if she lived close by. She just kept talking, with no sound. I told her I couldn't hear her. I felt helpless. The phone rang and when I turned back to her; she was gone.

My mind pushed this off as a freak encounter, thinking maybe I had left the door open and she had wandered in. Still, she disappeared so quickly and she made no sound. I was unsettled. A few weeks later, we were having a family night in front of the TV. All the doors were locked. I left the living room to grab refreshments from the kitchen and when I rounded the corner, there she was again, standing in my dining room. A sliver of wet fear slithered its way up the back of my neck. There she was, talking, with no sound, in the middle of my house. I whispered to her... "Are you ok?... Who are you?....." Deep down I was beginning to realize exactly who she was. I stood there trying to figure out what to do next. I closed my eyes and took a deep breath. When I opened them, she was gone. She was a hallucination and I was going absolutely crazy. It was in this instant, that the gripping fear that they were going to lock me away forever, took hold. I told no one and had no idea what to make of any of this. I consider myself to be an intelligent guy, so thoughts started creeping in... 'Is any of this real? How do I know what's happening is actually happening?' Will this last forever?'

She kept appearing, both inside and outside of the house. I remember working all day with her standing by my desk. The voices started too. Most of them were innocuous. I call them murmurs. I still struggle with them to this day. I remember the first time I heard them. I was sitting in the living room working out some new songs on my guitar. Suddenly, it sounded like there were a bunch of people talking in the other room. I couldn't make out what they were saying because the voices were so muffled. I went to the other room, and then they sounded like they were upstairs. They kept moving; I kept looking. Eventually, I realized what was happening, and just sat there shaking, not knowing quite what to do.

From the very beginning, the hallucinations fooled me. They still do, but my realization comes more quickly now. Yet, I am still tricked every time. It is similar to when you are dreaming. No matter how outlandish the dream is, you accept it as reality while you are in it. It is not until you wake up, you realize it was only a dream.

When hallucinations first appear, my rational brain does not engage, and I am completely deceived. After a while, even though the hallucination is still happening, I am better able to recognize it for what it is. It certainly doesn't make it any easier, trying to navigate the 'real' world with all that going on, but it allows me to utilize coping mechanisms to make it more manageable.

Up until the time the hallucinations first began, I was running more and more, averaging 100 miles a week. I was also running marathons and even did one 50-mile race. I recognize now that my obsession with running was a form of avoidance behavior. I used it to keep my distance, literally and figuratively. I felt free when I was running, especially on my long runs. When the hallucinations started, my running halted quickly. I was having trouble leaving the house regularly. I was afraid of what or who might 'show up' while I was out there. I couldn't run much at all after that. I was a prisoner to my own mind.

Other voices were extremely annoying. There was the man who would describe obscure tasks in great detail, such as how to install the blower fan on a furnace. He would go on and on in a monotone voice for hours. I was ready to drill holes in my head to get him to stop. I eventually named him Fred. Another voice was much more insidious and intrusive. His name was Drake. His voice was dark, loud, abusive, and reminded me of my mother, not in the sound of his voice, but in the tone and self-destructive nature of his words. His voice was the one that drove me to my suicide attempt. Each of them is difficult and penetrating in its own way.

No matter what form it takes, Schizophrenia is hard. One of the most challenging aspects is that I am never quite certain if I am seeing or hearing something that isn't there. It is unsettling. Everyone in the room is going about their business, unaware of what is happening to me. At this tragic turning point in my young adult life, my world was slowly unraveling. It made me feel that maybe my mother was right. I am damaged. I am broken.

6

PARENTHOOD

Your children are not your children.
They are the sons and daughters of Life's longing for itself.

Kahlil Gibran

Until my schizophrenia started, life was pretty good for me as a young adult. I had a good job, a happy marriage, and two beautiful little girls. We used to have whatever they wanted for dinner on their birthdays. One year, MarKatie proudly declared "Pancakes and mashed potatoes!" Pancakes and mashed potatoes it was and it was delicious. I will always remember their joy upon seeing the boot prints from Santa across the floor on Christmas morning. I remember taking them to the park often. Periodically they would fall, and to make them giggle instead of cry, I would say, "If the bones not showin', you keep goin'!" This would attract alarming looks from the other parents but it made the girls forget about their scraped knees. These are moments I carry with me to this very day.

One memory is still vivid in my mind. I had been called into work in the middle of the night and came home right before dawn. When I arrived home early the next morning, my oldest daughter was the only one awake. I knew from my long runs in the state park that the deer were often active this time of day. I bundled her up and put her in the car. Before long, we were lying in the grass, watching four beautiful deer wander along the tree line. It was a magical moment.

I was trying to be a good husband and father, but it often felt like I was just going through the motions, doing what I thought I was supposed to do. In the back of my mind, I suppose I was making sure I didn't do or say any of the things that my mother did. I loved my family. I told them I loved them. In reality, no one was truly close to me. On the outside, I was loving, but inside, everyone was at arm's length. I desperately wanted a life that was reminiscent of the bonds that poets write about, but I was afraid. Fear ruled me still. Everything in me told me I was broken and unlovable. I was certain that if I let anyone in, they would see how ugly I was deep inside, and I would be abandoned and shattered all over again. I felt like I was walking on eggshells, but now I realize I was the one who put them there. I spent a lot of time working and long-distance running, which kept me away from my family for longer and longer periods.

As I mentioned before, running was something I took to the extreme. Running an average of 100 miles a week, I was gone for over an hour almost every day. On Sundays, I ran 30 miles, so I was absent for half the day. Living in Wisconsin and running outside year-round, made this obsession even more extreme and potentially dangerous. My drive for self-isolation was so intense that I would be out there for hours in the sub-zero darkness of the Northern winters.

I am very aware now of what a tremendous sacrifice this placed upon my family. I have deep regrets about this period in my life. I wish more than ever I could have those hours back with my wife and children. As I reflect on my family life, I am saddened by the tragic truth that my children essentially grew up without me.

Many people who suffer from trauma, especially in their childhood, grow up with an ever-present void inside of them. Some choose to fill this hole with alcohol and drugs, unhealthy relationships, material things, etc. I filled mine with running. With the intensity of my running and a very busy work schedule, I rarely spent quality time with my family. I was empty inside, and instead of turning to the people in my life for help, support, and fulfillment, I ran. I was literally running away.

Two years before my son was born, with a three-year-old and a one-year-old at home, my life changed forever. That day alone in the house when the young girl appeared and was talking with no sound, the day 'Claire' decided to show up, is a day I will never forget. I went from a life of isolation to the haunting possibility that someone might invade my space at any time, no matter where I was.

I'm going to say that again.

I went from a life of isolation to the haunting possibility that someone might invade my space at any time, no matter where I was.

Life slowly began to unravel in front of me. I was reluctant to tell anyone, much less seek help because I was sure that they would put me in a mental hospital for the rest of my life. I was working more, although this got to be tougher as my hallucinations increased in frequency. I drank more and my wife noticed. I was very distant and found it difficult to deal with the events of everyday life. Even going to the store became challenging. I struggled with paranoia as well. I was convinced everyone I encountered was reading my thoughts or part of an elaborate conspiracy against me.

I did as much research as I could about my hallucinations. There wasn't much out there at the time. What I found wasn't consistent. The internet was still in the infantile stage, so access to information was limited. I quickly discovered that the diagnosis and treatment of schizophrenia varied greatly and was mostly not understood very well. Even decades later, the illness is still widely misunderstood.

Modern media and television have not helped to foster education about it. In contrast, they have created a horrifically negative stigma around it. My hope in writing this book is to open a dialogue that will facilitate growth and understanding. One that will foster change, not only with those who struggle to cope with its' daunting grasp but for everyone else as well.

7

ONE WAY TICKET

The only thing we have to fear is fear itself.

Franklin D. Roosevelt

On a routine business trip, I was in the airport getting ready to make the short flight home. The company's headquarters was in Minneapolis, so I traveled there regularly. It had been a long day in the lab. Before preparing to board the plane, I made a quick stop by the restroom and sat in the stall. Two men came in and I knew instantly they were pilots. They were discussing control panels, flight plans, and other relevant topics related to flying. Suddenly, they started talking about my flight – and about ME specifically. They said that they had orders to divert the flight to Chicago so I could be taken to a hospital because I was having dangerous symptoms.

I was frozen with fear. I had my feet up on the door so they wouldn't see me. I also thought this would make it harder for them to get in if they decided to. I was shaking uncontrollably. I was gritting my teeth and clenching my fists so hard that I never heard the end of their conversation. I don't even remember them leaving the restroom. I stayed there for a long time. I missed my flight by what must have been hours.

I finally mustered up enough courage to leave the restroom. It was late because the airport was in night mode. I am guessing it was around midnight. My cell phone was off. I had almost submerged it in the toilet and left it behind, but something told me to keep it. When I eventually left the airport, it took me a while to orient myself and find my way out of the inner roads and parking lots. I wandered around until I found a big tree and sat under it for quite some time, contemplating how in the world someone would have found out about what was going on with me. I knew that whatever happened, I needed to make sure I didn't get caught. Being in an airport filled with cameras was no place to be. I left the security of the large tree and made my way out onto the streets of Minneapolis. I was hungry but didn't dare go to a diner or restaurant. I thought about going to a convenience store, but I had no cash, and I was positive that all of my credit cards were being tracked.

Eventually, I came upon a large open park, with lots of covered tables. It was a summer night, so I made my way to one of them away from the road so I could gather my thoughts. My mind was racing. I couldn't figure out what was happening and was convinced the authorities were going to come out of the night at any second. I did some deep breathing and eventually was able to calm down and slow my racing mind. I must have been completely exhausted from the terror of the night because I fell asleep on top of the table.

I awoke to the sun shining and the warmth hitting my face. For a few moments, I had no idea where I was. I was disoriented, and then suddenly I remembered. The paranoia of the previous night had faded, and I knew enough about my hallucinations to know that I must have imagined everything the pilots were saying in the restroom. There was no way to know if they had been there at all. My rational mind had returned. I needed to get home. I headed out of the park towards the airport. On the way there I turned my cell phone back on. I had countless missed calls and voicemails from my wife. She was terribly worried since my bag had arrived, but I had not. Her last message said that if she didn't hear from me by the morning, she was calling the police.

I called her as soon as I returned to the airport. I explained that I had fallen asleep in the airport, missed my flight, and had only now just woken up. She went into a long explanation of how scared she was and that I had been acting strangely recently. She subtly hinted at the possibility of something else going on. I told her again that I had fallen asleep and apologized for worrying her. What else could I do? Nobody knew what was going on with me. I was conditioned to keep all my troubles to myself from a very early age. It was like being in hell, except hell was all inside my head. I couldn't let anybody else know I was there. I was in that closet all over again.

When I returned home that afternoon, it was the beginning of the end. My avoidance behavior and strange actions had escalated to the point she thought I was having an affair. With everything that was happening, that was certainly the last thing on my mind, but I was too confused and scared to tell her the truth.

8

HEAVY DAYS

Lost time is never found again.

Benjamin Franklin

I was barely holding it together and had no idea what to do. Paranoid delusions about people at work began to haunt me, so I missed a lot of work. Home was no refuge; I was constantly making up excuses or lying about why I was acting in a certain way. Claire persisted in coming, and now Fred had joined her. He wore crazy suits and was very energetic. He would run around yelling and throwing things. It was impossible to concentrate and not react. I did anything I could to be alone when he was there. I drank more. I found it increasingly difficult to be around anyone – even my own family. Eventually, things spiraled out of control. My wife asked me to find my own place for the sake of the children. I was devastated, even though a part of me was relieved.

I found a small apartment close to my new job. I had changed jobs around that time because I was no longer able to travel and feel safe. At first, it was nice, not having to pretend I was okay when all hell was breaking loose around me. The kids did visit, and I did my best to be a fun dad and do things with them, but video games and movies quickly became the norm. The relentless torment of my mother's voice in my head plagued me – especially related to parenting. Rowdiness and noise were intolerable. It was difficult to even be around the interaction of them 'just being kids.' I drank more, which shortened my fuse. I never hit them, but I certainly yelled and stormed around quite often. Unbeknownst to me at the time, I was reacting the same way my mother had so many years ago. It was in no way an excuse for my bad behavior, but an element of growth that wasn't presented to me until recently. I am grateful I have been given the chance to rewrite the narrative that was playing in my head back then, but I regret I didn't have the insight to correct it sooner.

Music quickly became my refuge again. If I wasn't working, I was playing my guitar or piano. Fred or Claire visited often and there were a lot of days the voices were so bad; that all I could do was play endlessly or lie on my bed in the dark with headphones.

Until the writing of this book, my first wife and children never knew the extent to which I was struggling. They knew I had changed a lot and that something was troubling me, but they never knew why. In silence, I languished in a personal hell that was difficult to navigate from one moment to the next. They did not know about my hallucinations back then, and to them, I randomly started drinking more and acting erratic. I was agitated easily and had zero patience. I isolated myself from the people who loved me the most. In doing so, I lost them.

This tragic outcome in my own life is one of the most important reasons I chose to write this book. I hope that I can help change the course of people's lives in a positive way. By reading my story, I hope others have the courage to open up to their loved ones. I hope they are brave enough to step into the light of their embrace much earlier than I did. If I had the strength to trust my wife with my pain, I would have saved myself and everyone in my life a tremendous amount of heartache and struggle.

Around this time, my now oldest friend Craig, came into the mix. He was a bass player and I was playing guitar. I had posted an ad in the local music shop, and he answered it. It wasn't long before we got together. I still remember our first jam session. We melded immediately, changing direction in sync like a school of fish as if we had been playing together for many years.

To Craig, I was zany and manic. Unpredictable and prone to bizarre behavior, I engaged with the world as a madman. I remember calling him over to give me a mohawk late one night. While he was there, I was reacting to all kinds of things in the room that weren't there. He had no idea what was causing my erratic behavior. I was drinking to compensate for everything that was happening, which caused me to act more and more schizoid.

One night we were on stage at a crowded bar, playing a rather rowdy version of my song, Little Visions. It is a driving funk tune, with a catchy guitar line. The excitement of the audience was steadily growing. I suddenly unstrapped my guitar, letting it fall with a loud bang, grabbed the microphone, and in a voice full of voltage sang "I am just an ordinary guy...BURNING DOWN THE HOUSE!!!!" The bar erupted in a drunken euphoria as the band raged on. People were lighting napkins on fire and tossing them into the currents of the ceiling fans.

I continued to miss more work. I went from a fun dad to a strange and distant dad. I lost my job. I took a job as a Buick brand manager at a car dealership. I missed a fair amount of work there too.

On top of all this, my dad was battling cancer and not doing well. I went down to visit him as frequently as I could, but it was hard seeing him that way. I still was unsure if he knew that my mother had put me in the closet all those years. He knew that our relationship wasn't the best, but I was doubtful that he knew about that. I couldn't bear the thought that he knew and didn't do anything. That would have been almost as bad, maybe worse.

I remember one visit to my parents' home. My father was sleeping, and my mother started in on me. Things escalated quickly as she was keen to point out my recent failures at work and with my family. I immediately got defensive and voices were raised. As it got louder and darker by the syllable, my mother yelled "You're killing your father!" Rationally I knew the cancer was not my fault, but the piercing tone and hurtful words of that statement lingered in my mind like a dagger for over a decade after he was gone.

9

THE CURSE

We only die once, and for such a long time.

Moliére

My dad and I spent his last days in hospice watching the Red Sox and their incredible comeback from 0-3 down against the dreaded Yankees in 2004. It was a time I will never forget, and it will forever be etched upon my soul. The first few games, I was crushed. I thought to myself, he has spent his whole life waiting for a championship, and we're losing it all to the Yankees again. Then in game 4, a miracle happened. My dad was asleep for most of the second half of the game, but he woke up in the extra innings to see the winning hit. I remember his thin smile and he reached out for my hand. I knew at that moment, there was a chance.

He stayed awake for the entire fifth game, even cheering quietly from time to time. The sixth game was interrupted because he was having trouble breathing. I watched every single play. I ran down the hall giving him updates whenever he was awake. Game seven, we celebrated. The entire game was the culmination of a lifetime's worth of frustration coming to life. We danced on their lawn. I couldn't believe it. The Red Sox were on their way to the World Series. Quietly, I hoped with all my might that he would get to see it happen.

We watched them win the World Series together, and shortly after that, he was gone. I was so happy he got to witness the 86-year curse be broken. I didn't want to make his final days stressful and conflicted, so I never got up the courage to ask him if he knew about the closet. We talked instead about traveling together to Austria, Scotland, and Ireland. We discussed anything but the elephant I was feeling in the room. Maybe he felt it, too. Ever since he passed, I have regretted not asking and wish I had. I've struggled with that so much. I want to believe he didn't know. He <u>did</u> know about the verbal abuse. He witnessed it and allowed it. There were times he intervened when my mother and I argued, but the verbal abuse continued.

It's a mystery to me why he didn't do more. It hurts and makes me feel even more alone in those years every time I think about it.

He passed away in November of 2004. I went to the funeral but did not sit with the family. I delivered the eulogy and left shortly after the service. For me, it was the end of my family. I was obviously not close to my mother, and my brother and I were too far apart in age to be tight. Although through no fault of his own, and for whatever reason, I was the one who was abused, and my brother was not. It created a separation between us that lasts to this very day. Other than my grandmother, my father was the only person with whom I ever had a relationship. Now they were gone. On the ride home that day, I knew there was no reason left for me to ever speak to that family again.

10

CRISIS

A man has no more character than he can command in a time of crisis.

Ralph W. Sockman

      Consciousness was evading me. I slowly came to...holding my phone like a prayer. Drake had been yelling at me relentlessly for over 12 hours. I don't know how many sleeping pills I took, but my only thought was to make him go away. I lay in that bed, wondering what would happen when I died. Would I be born again? Would I go somewhere? Would people be mad? Sad? I could feel my body shutting down. It was getting hard to breathe. I panicked. With every ounce of will I had left I unlocked my phone and dialed 911.

      I was rushed to the hospital and treated quickly. After what had happened, they checked me into the mental health ward. Despite all my efforts, I ended up there anyway. A doctor came in, wondering why I had tried to take my own life. I said that I was losing my job and wouldn't be able to afford my apartment much longer. I told him I felt like a bad father and husband. I didn't say a word about my schizophrenia. Not a single word. I said anything except to admit what was happening in my head. I don't think he bought what I was telling him. The way I conveyed it was very stoic and unemotional. Regardless of what he speculated might be going on, after a few days, I was released from the hospital. I did not go back to my apartment. I was sent to a group home in town, where I could stabilize and be sure to take my new medication under supervision.

      The meds seemed to calm my racing thoughts a little but did absolutely nothing for the hallucinations. It makes sense now why they didn't work. I only had myself to blame because I never told anyone what was really going on. If you break your leg but go to the ER and say your arm hurts, you're not going to get the care you need. At first, I was very paranoid about being at the group home. I kept totally to myself, was reticent in groups, and isolated myself in my room. Thankfully my roommate was never in there, except to sleep, so I had our room to myself.

Looking back, what I needed was someone to talk to, but I wasn't ready for that yet. It was hard. I felt like a failure - as a father, a son, and as a person. I worried about what was happening to all the things in my apartment, and if I would still have employment. Instead of focusing on getting better and accepting the help that was offered me, I was preoccupied with the swirling thoughts in my head. Worry and fear whirled around like a cyclone full of torn bits of paper. When I slept, I had horrible nightmares. Nightmares about being in the closet, about the hallucinations becoming physical, and about being homeless. Ironically, in a short amount of time, that's exactly what I would become.

My mother would visit me in the group home periodically. I did not look forward to her visits. I could not only see the disappointment in her eyes, I had to endure hearing it from her mouth. "I told you that you were going to be a failure." "Look at you, what are you going to do when they kick you out of here? Live on the streets?" It was agonizing. I was in a bad place already, and now here I was with my only visitor reminding me of all that was terrible in my world, relentlessly kicking me while I was down.

We went to lunch periodically. One day in the winter, we went to Subway. She started in as soon as we sat down to eat. Finally, I slammed my fist down on the table and left. It was very cold, but I walked the four miles back to the group home. I was so angry I didn't even feel the sting of the Northern wind.

The next day I was in a session with my therapist. I said, "She really knows how to push my buttons." The therapist looked at me, and very calmly said, "What are your buttons?" Chills are running up my arms as I recall this distinct memory. It was such a profound moment. I had no idea what my buttons were. I walked out of that session consumed by this thought. It completely changed my interactions with my mother. I didn't really, but in a way, I almost looked *forward* to her coming. Every encounter was another chance to unlock this new puzzle.

I remember a visit shortly after this in which she launched into a demeaning monologue about my future, and how I needed to get back on my feet or I was going to end up going through the garbage. She was barking, and suddenly, I realized that by highlighting my insecurities, she was trying to diminish her own. I started laughing right in the middle of it. She stopped and looked like I had just slapped her across the face. That was the true beginning of my departure from where I had been, to where I was going.

From the very beginning of the onset of my hallucinations, three main ones persisted. Lesli suggested the possibility they could be a manifestation of imagos that represented aspects of my life. Claire was the first. She represented me as a child, unable to speak or express my feelings. She had plenty to say, but no sound could be heard because no one listened. Drake is certainly the worst, and quite clearly represented the unrelenting pejorative voice of my mother. I'm not certain about Fred, but he could be the impulsive side of my manic episodes poking through.

Learning to deal with them in a non-destructive way was the most important thing. I knew I needed help but was still not prepared to share the truth about what was happening.

11

DUALITY

*We are more often frightened than hurt;
and we suffer more from imagination than from reality.*

Seneca

I met a woman at the group home named Lana. She was about my age and struggled with Schizophrenia. Our casual friendship never developed into anything but at times it was clear that she wanted it to. I was diligently keeping my distance from every soul on Earth and had no intention of changing that bearing. We would often have discussions about our illness over terrible decaf coffee (they denied us the good stuff). I don't remember much about her except that she was unpredictable in her social interactions. Sometimes, she would talk to me all day every single day for a while, and then she would shift and sit quietly for days with nothing to say. I didn't take it personally; everybody there was dealing with a lot.

Lana got out of the group home before I did and went to live with her mom. She called a couple of times and talked about various things, including her children. I remember her suggesting that she wanted to get together when I got out. I didn't have any interest in that, but I was polite about letting her know.

One night she called. I remember there being a heavy storm raging outside the windows. I sat in the day room on the chair by the phone (we weren't allowed cell phones either), and half-listened while she talked about her day of taking her two toddlers to the apple orchard. I could hear them playing and laughing in the background. She seemed happy and content. It all seemed innocuous enough, and after a while, my time was up. We said goodnight, and that was it.

The next day two detectives showed up. When the police show up at a group home, it causes quite a panic. I was in the minority and wasn't freaking out. Not at first anyway, until I realized they wanted to talk to ME. We made our way to my room and one of them shut the door. I must have had a terrified look on my face because one of them said, "It's okay Todd, you've done nothing wrong, we just have a few questions for you." That made me feel a little better, but my heart was still racing. They started asking about Lana. I told them about our benign relations and that we had spoken a couple of times since she left. Finally, they zeroed in on the call from the night before.

They asked, "Did she say anything strange? How was her tone? Did she laugh?" I told them as much as I could remember but admitted to them, I was only half listening. The sweet little voices and laughter of her children echoed in my head. Suddenly, the officers dropped the bombshell. Lana had been up late that night reading the Bible. Apparently, God had spoken to her and told her to kill her children. She obediently smothered both of them while they slept. They said she was dry and a matter of fact when she told them what she had done, like she was making toast or something. I think my heart skipped a beat and I said something like "Oh my God...."

They asked me not to tell anyone about what they had said but thought I should know in case she tried to call me from the prison. I told them that I would most definitely be declining her calls. I had to document and write out a few things about the call. They gave me a business card in case I thought of anything else, and then they left. It wasn't until after they were gone; that it suddenly hit me. I nearly collapsed.

Lana is a schizophrenic. I am a schizophrenic.

She had young children. I have young children.

I could do what she did.

Something in me changed forever in that thought. I didn't know how, but I had to do whatever I could to ensure that I didn't hurt anyone. Not just my kids, but anyone.

12

BREAKING AWAY

The clearest way into the Universe is through a forest wilderness.

John Muir

After 3 months, I was released from the group home. Those last few months were filled with an ever-present, ominous dark cloud hovering over me. We were allowed two weekly trips to the library. I spent every second of that time reading everything I could about wilderness survival. Aside from grave thoughts of suicide, it was the only path I could imagine that would ensure I didn't hurt anyone. I had some money saved away, mostly from when I was working, but also from doing odd jobs like raking leaves and painting around the group home. I had spent every waking moment preparing. As I left the group home, I made my way to an outdoor/camping store. My scrutinized list was planned to the letter so I wasn't in there very long. It was early spring in Wisconsin, so it was still relatively cold. In the weeks prior, I had scouted out an unoccupied woodsy area near the store. I spent my first night homeless there. I didn't sleep at all.

The next morning, in early April, strapped down with a heavy pack, I walked away. I refused to be a burden to anyone. I was constantly haunted by the fear of being put in an institution if anyone found out what was happening. Above anything else, I didn't want to do what Lana had done, or anything even close to it. I headed South.

The first thing I missed was the comfort of a bed. The second was walls and a roof. I had decided to go primitive and not get a tent. Instead, I invested in a nice pair of boots. I carried two tarps, one for above and one for below. I was confident in my ability to make my own shelters, and besides, two brown tarps were not only a lot lighter to carry but could be set up or taken down quickly. I was still pretty paranoid about being found, so tarps were a lot easier to conceal in the woods than the unmistakable profile of a tent. It didn't take long for my survival skills reading to pay off. Somewhere around the Wisconsin/Illinois border, on the fourth or fifth night out, I caught my first rabbit. I had set some snare traps earlier in the day. I was fairly confident I knew what I was doing, but I was still uncertain. After a childhood of always being doubted, it was hard to shake that feeling.

Around dusk that evening, I went out to check my traps. As I approached the last one, there it was - my first rabbit. I promptly took it back to my camp, cleaned it, and cooked it. After nearly a week of noodles and peanut butter, it tasted amazing. I was starting to believe I could do this. This was possible. Maybe if I stayed out here long enough, away from society, the hallucinations would fall away. Maybe. All I had was hope and a pack full of stuff.

I quickly learned that just because I had left the world behind, did not mean my struggles with schizophrenia wouldn't follow me. I struggled daily with daunting symptoms. One day Fred would be running around as I walked. Another day, Claire would appear around each new turn I took. Lurking murmurs and strange people in fields off to the side of the road would startle me. I kept walking.

13

AN UNEXPECTED STORY

*Being deeply loved by someone gives you strength,
while loving someone deeply gives you courage.*

Lao Tzu

I made my way to Cordova Illinois. I arrived at dawn and found a small park on the banks of the Mississippi River. I laid down in the grass by the water, using my pack as a headrest, and quickly fell asleep. After a while, I awoke to raindrops on my face. I gathered my things and moved to the only shelter available. I was only there for a few moments when a rickety Datsun pickup pulled up. Out rambled a short, portly man with white hair and a mustache. I immediately thought of the Monopoly man.

He came up and asked, "Where are you from?" I told him and he introduced himself as George. After talking for a bit, he invited me to lunch at his house. I had a good feeling about him, so I accepted. We hopped in his Datsun and made our way back to his home. When we arrived, he announced, "Ida we have company." She immediately appeared and with a quick hello and a wholesome smile, started preparing lunch.

George was shorter than Ida, but this juxtaposition seemed to fit them well. Ida was stoic, measured in her responses, and her hands were busy, like birds in the cold. George was more sedentary and ran his hand through his white hair often. It framed his face like a house with a fresh blanket of snow.

George pulled out all his maps and we started looking over my possible route. Eventually, Ida came by and was curious. I interrupted our plans suddenly and blurted out, "How did you two meet?" Ida immediately stepped back, and George smiled like a school kid who had just scored Joe DiMaggio's rookie card. Quietly, Ida began... "I was 16 and I went to visit a friend. When I got to her house, she was on her bed writing a letter to her boyfriend who was in the war. I remember saying to her that I wished I had someone to write to. She replied, "Well, his bunkmate's name is George."

Upon this statement, Ida left the room. George picked up the story, saying that he got her letter, amid absolute chaos and death. It was his absolute. He was a tank mechanic and saw his fair share of the ruins of combat. He recalled an incident where a tank came in damaged from a grenade. They were pulling dead soldiers out while he began repairing the tread. Ida immediately became his link to a world of hope, his lifeline. He wrote back.

It was about this time that Ida returned. She was carrying a large oak box. She set it down in front of me, saying simply "Have a look...." Carefully, I opened the lid. Inside, was every note they had ever written to each other, in order. Hers were all on perfumed stationery and his were on the back of tank manuals, or any sort of paper he could get his hands on. They were still marred and smelling of grease and blood. I started to weep. We all started to weep.

It was at this time that Ida spoke up. "I was so young, but somehow felt like I knew George better than anyone I ever would. I convinced my parents to drive me to Indiana to meet him in person when he got off the plane. I remember being so nervous, standing there..."

"She was so radiant and beautiful," George said, reaching out for her hand. "I knew that she was the girl for me. Without hesitation, and without saying another word, I walked up to her, took a knee, and asked her to be my wife."

We sat in silence for a few moments. I looked at the two of them, a model of love in its simplest and most complete dressings. Not so much for myself, but for the world, they gave me hope.

Evening was quickly approaching, and I needed to figure out where I was going to camp that night. I wouldn't have stayed with them even if they had asked. I made pleasantries and thanked them for everything, especially for their story. I climbed back in the old dusty Datsun pickup truck and George drove me back to where he found me. Suddenly, after a solid handshake, I was alone again.

14

AFTER THE STORM

Nothing brings me more happiness than trying to help the most vulnerable people. It is a goal and an essential part of my life – a kind of destiny. Whoever is in distress can call on me. I will come running wherever they are.

Princess Diana

    I yearned for mountains and big skies. As I made my way through Missouri and Nebraska life distilled itself to a very simple existence. I walked, I ate, I made camp, and I walked again. I lived by the clock of the sun. I had no electronic devices whatsoever, except my headlamp - no watch, no radio, no phone. I started to discover life at three miles per hour. It was very soothing. I still hallucinated and had rabid paranoia, but I didn't have to hide it from anyone anymore. I could talk back as I was walking along or lying in my shelter, and nobody was there to think anything about it. I took up the pastime of throwing rocks at Claire and Fred. Sometimes they would bounce off, and sometimes they would pass right through. In a big way, that made it easier. It was still hard, but not quite as much.

    I spent a lot of time thinking about my kids, wondering what they had been told and how worried they were. My heart ached for them every day, but I knew they were safe. I knew they were safe from me. Life evaporated itself down into the simplest of activities. Isolation settled in as I rarely had any contact with people. People would see me as they drove by, but days and weeks went by without talking to anyone. I wasn't used to that at first, but as time went on, I became more accustomed to being alone.

    I would make up stories about who I was, where I had come from, and why I was out here. They ranged from the mundane to the unbelievable. I would just walk along, occupying my mind by creating all of them in elaborate detail. It gave me something to do and served to comfort me so I would have a story other than schizophrenia, suicide attempt, and group home to tell someone if they stopped to ask what I was doing.

In Missouri, I survived a rather bad storm one night. The next morning, I packed up and headed out along a country road. As I was walking, I saw an elderly woman and two little boys on the front porch of a trailer home. The roof had partially collapsed during the storm, and they were trying to re-pitch it. It wasn't going well. The young boys were only around five and the woman was very short. They couldn't reach the area of the roof and it looked like a lost cause.

I quickly turned down the driveway, and as I approached, I drew their attention away, saying "Can I help?" I am almost six feet tall so I knew my height would be advantageous. The woman smiled, holding onto one of the boys, who was standing on the railing with a hammer, still not able to reach the top of the post. "By golly yes young man!!!" I got close and introduced myself. Harriet introduced Devon and Sean, and I took the hammer and got to work.

Her face was round, with beaming eyes that were small only in their size. The light that radiated from them told decades of stories, joy, and loss. For a moment, we locked our eyes and there was an understanding. We were good people here. Good people are helpful. There was an unspoken trust as solid as the lines around her timeless smile.

Before too long, the porch roof was fixed, and Harriet was completely grateful. Her eyes sparkled brightly contrasted against her dark skin, and she insisted that I stay for dinner. It was a wonderful meal, very Southern, with baked chicken, grits, beans, and pie to finish. It was amazing. I told a few stories about my travels, which hadn't been much to this point, but Harriet hung on every word. I was still surprised at how trusting everyone was, and how comfortable I was feeling. I stayed the night and slept on an old leather couch in the living room.

In the morning, Harriet informed me it was Sunday, and I was coming to church, so she could thank the Lord for me and my help. I could not refuse. She was so sincere. I graciously accepted but let her know I had no church clothes in my bag. Harriet returned promptly with a dark suit that had belonged to her late husband. It seemed freshly pressed like she knew I would be coming.

I ventured to the bathroom to change but quickly discovered that Harriet's husband must have been seven feet tall. The sleeves of the shirt and jacket hung over my hands like seal flippers, and the pants and shoes were so oversized, that they looked silly. When I came out, she smiled and pinned up the pants as best she could. I had to keep my arms at an angle, so the sleeves didn't hang down so much.

On the ride to the church, we were talking about different parts of our lives. At one point I asked her, "What was the most impactful invention during your life?" I figured she would say something like computers, satellites, or the internet. To my surprise, she said, "Screens."

"Like for computers?"

Her laugh was delightful and free, like a brook flowing over round stones.

"No silly, screens for the windows of your house."

She explained that when she was a young girl growing up in Kansas their house was incredibly hot. You couldn't open a window unless you wanted all the bugs to come in. One day a salesman came down the road and sold them screens to nail up over their windows.

"It changed my life!"

It truly is the small things in life that matter the most.

We arrived at a small Baptist church, off the side of a road. Cars were parked in all different directions. She found a spot and we went in. I realized instantly that I was the only white person there. Just as quickly, I knew I was completely welcome. Everyone seemed to already know what had happened with the porch. The singing was out of this world, and I had a delightful time clapping along with my seal flipper suit. After the service, she introduced me to more people, and then we piled in her old station wagon and headed back to their home. I changed, and when I went to gather my pack, Harriet was crying. I could tell she wasn't sad, just hopeful, as she wished me "a most safe and satisfying journey." Before too long, I was on my way, heading West and North.

I had been traveling for some time but had lost track of days and wasn't sure if it was June or July. I wandered into a truck stop in Nebraska. Nebraska had been tough. Water was scarce and there was a lot of barbed wire and very few treed areas to camp. I slept under a lot of bridges. Often, I would just wrap myself up like a burrito and lay down in a deep ditch until morning. I was craving a shower. It had been several months since I had felt anything but cold creeks and lakes upon my skin. I paid my five dollars at the truck stop and boy did I get my money's worth out of that shower. I must have been in there for an hour. I can't elucidate the feeling of warm water after months of its absence. It truly was so heavenly I felt like calling out. I didn't though, I was worried they would think something nefarious was going on in there.

After my glorious shower, I treated myself to a bag of chips and cold water. I sat down in the restaurant and was immediately struck by how odd it felt to sit in a chair. It had been months of sitting on the ground. The lights and noises of people coming and going were also somewhat alarming. Just being in a big structure was unsettling in a way. Part of me wanted to head home, to be surrounded again by the comforts of life. At the same time, every nerve in my body was screaming to get the hell out of there. It is hard to describe. I suppose it would be similar to being housebound by yourself and then suddenly taken from that refuge and placed in Times Square. That may seem extreme, but that's how it felt. I felt completely exposed and out of my element. My paranoia was kicking in. I was sure everyone was talking about me, getting ready to call the cops or worse. My brain was trapped in that cyclone all over again.

I left in a big hurry, and it took me quite a while to settle down once I got outside. I desperately longed for headphones and music. I think I missed that more than food and shelter.

15

DEPARTURE

*Leaving home in a sense involves a kind of
second birth in which we give birth to ourselves.*

Robert Neelly Bellah

Later, I was sitting outside on the grass by my pack when an older man with boots, a belt buckle, and a big gray mustache approached. He asked where I was headed.

"West for now, not sure, just want to see some mountains."

"You set on walking that whole way?" he said with a wry grin.

"Well, I guess, not sure..."

"You might be in luck; I'm headed straight through to Boise. I could use the company, and I can tell by the look of that pack that you've been out here for long enough to have some stories."

"Um, yeah sure, that would be good, thanks" I couldn't get over how much he looked like he had just stepped out of a western. He was missing the hat, but the big mustache and bushy eyebrows both wiggled when he talked. In a way, it was comforting to watch his face. His teeth were stained from midnight drives chugging black coffee.

I wasn't sure at all about riding with a stranger all that way, especially since my social skills appeared to be severely handicapped. I was uncertain about whether I could do it but I decided I could make an excuse and just get out at any time if I needed to. Besides, I knew I didn't want to walk through the rest of Nebraska. If you have ever driven through there you can only imagine what it would be like on foot. I stood up and started to grab my pack.

"Now hold on there youngin...I just got done driving for ten hours. If you are still here at this spot at 7 a.m. sharp, I'll take you the whole way."

"Deal," I said, and we shook hands. Now I just had to make sure I didn't sleep past seven. With no watch, that was going to be difficult. I also had no idea where I was going to sleep.

I found a secluded spot behind the truck stop, fired up my stove, and had some noodles. After dinner, I read for a while and started to get drowsy. I wasn't sure quite what to do. I went for a walk, looking at all the big rigs, realizing that I had never ridden in one before. I knew that by the time Orion's belt lined up East and West, I had about two hours to go. I watched the stars for a while and kept taking intermittent walks. Right about the time the belt lined up, I was starting to get sleepy again. I had an idea. I went in and filled my water bottles. I also bought a small coffee. I drank both bottles and the coffee in short order. It was only about 30-45 minutes before I had to go to the bathroom. My idea was not to go. I knew that falling asleep would be next to impossible if I had to pee. It worked. The sun came up, and I went in to check the time and finally relieve my bladder. It was 6:25. I wandered around in the store for a while looking at all the corny T-shirts and bumper stickers. Eventually, I made my way to our meeting spot, and there he came, right on time.

"Reckon I could set a watch by you son." He said playfully.

"Thanks, you too, my name is Todd, by the way."

"Walter. Right, good, you ready to go?"

"Absolutely!"

In the back of my mind, I was a little worried about him getting weird or kidnapping me, but I was carrying several knives and had a good feeling about him. I had never been in a semi before. It was an empowering sensation to be up that high. The whole thing shook when we started. It took much longer than a car, but soon we were up to speed, and the scenery was rolling by. I had no idea, but it was making me anxious. I was safe, there was music, and the hard-to-trek plains were passing by without effort. I finally realized I hadn't gone faster than a walking pace for several months. Once that fact settled in my mind, I started to focus on the music. Stairway to Heaven was playing. I was never much of a classic rock fan, but after all that time with nothing but silence, I was grateful for it. At some point, I fell asleep. When I woke up, we were parked at a rest area and Walter was in the sleeper section snoring.

The trip was relatively uneventful. We shared our stories and talked about baseball. The last day was another story.

We woke up and went in for breakfast at the truck stop. We were only a few hours from Boise, which was the end of the line for me. I was just about to tell Walter that I had enjoyed his company and that I would miss our talks when the voices kicked in. At first, I thought there was a large table of people that had suddenly come in behind us. I looked but nobody was there. Then suddenly, it sounded like they were coming from over by the hallway near the bathrooms. I couldn't figure out what was going on at first. Eventually, the realization that I was having a hallucination set in. I spent the rest of breakfast and the final leg of our trip trying to act as if nothing was wrong. It was extremely difficult to carry on a conversation with Walter because at times the voices were very loud. I think he sensed that something was going on because he asked me a couple of times if I was feeling alright. I said I was okay and made the excuse that I wasn't used to being around people. I assured him that I was enjoying our time but hadn't talked to anyone for a long time.

Those last few hours of our trip seemed to last forever. I was trying to enjoy the company and the scenery, but the voices were getting louder. There were many moments when I almost shouted for him to stop. I wanted to just get out. I didn't know what else to do, but in the end, I kept quiet. Finally, as we were approaching the city, Walter said, "I'm going to stop and let you off somewhere soon, I can't take you to my drop."

"That's okay, anywhere will do."

We took an exit and pulled into the back section of a Walmart parking lot. I thanked Walter tremendously for everything and wished him well. I wanted to say more, but the voices were loud. He also seemed like he needed to keep moving, so it all worked out. I climbed down from the rig and shut the door. Walter roared it back to life and off he went.

It was midday, and I wasn't quite sure what to do. I could see the mountains in the far distance, and desperately wanted to go there immediately. At the same time, I knew this might be my last chance to buy needed supplies. Still, the thought of going into a busy Walmart with voices was difficult to imagine.

I sat for a while on the grass at the back edge of the parking lot, staring at the mountains and making a mental inventory of my supplies. I wanted to live off the land as much as possible and felt prepared to do so. Everything was in full bloom, so there would be plenty of plants and berries. I had also gotten quite adept at trapping rabbits. I was trying to decide if I could make it out of the city before dark and find a place to camp. What were my other options? I could hang out here all night, but I might get hassled by the police. I could try and find a city park with trees. I wasn't sure what to do. After a little while, I gathered up my courage and headed into the store for a few things. I would then book it out of town before it started to get dark.

The voices were loud, but I focused on what I was doing. I was trying not to react to them, which would cause other shoppers to notice me. I had my big pack in the shopping cart, so that was drawing enough attention on its own. I bought some paracord, a big jar of peanut butter, some beef jerky to fuel me for my journey out of town, and a few other little things. I was very weight-conscious, and my pack was stuffed with supplies. I left the store around two and headed for the hills. I was finally bound for directly for the Sawtooth Mountains.

16

FORTITUDE

*Out of suffering have emerged the strongest souls;
the most massive characters are seared with scars.*

Khalil Gibran

I made it out of town and was on a winding country highway when a car slowed and the window came down. It was a woman, maybe ten years older than me, with a young girl in the back seat.

"Headed to the mountains?"

"I sure am!"

"How long are you going for?"

I had learned that this question could cause alarm if answered honestly.

"Couple of weeks..."

"Well, take care of yourself and stay safe."

"Thanks, I sure will."

With that, she drove off. About 30 minutes later, I saw her going back the other way towards town. She waved and I smiled. The scenery here was delightful. My voices were fading, and I was almost able to completely enjoy the mountain air and vistas that people write about in books. I was really doing it. I was out there, doing what I felt I had to do. I certainly felt as if I...

Her car pulled up again and the window came down. I was alarmed.

"Here you go, last meal before the woods!"

She handed me a McDonalds bag, smiled, and zoomed away. I stopped, not sure what to think. I looked in the bag and there were two cheeseburgers, fries, and a can of Pepsi. I found a spot off the road and savored every molecule of that meal. I was grateful, and I was ready. A few miles further down the road, I came upon a park service sign for the Sawtooth National Forest. I turned there, intent on finding a station or a store with a map.

I found a nice, wooded area near a stream and made camp. It was quiet, with the soothing sound of the stream lulling me to sleep. I slept well that night. It was clear, and I remember the moon being mostly full. I had no idea what was in store or what would become of me. I just knew that at that very moment, I was safe, and so was everyone else.

I woke the next morning before dawn and guessed by the position of Orion's belt it was about an hour before sunrise. I had found some watercress near my campsite, so I enjoyed breakfast with a handful of that, oatmeal, and a few spoonfuls of peanut butter. As I was finishing my meal, the sky was light enough for me to safely walk along the shoulder of the highway. I headed out, full of excitement and a little bit of trepidation. I knew where I was going if something happened, there would be nobody driving along to rescue me if something happened. I was heading towards true and utter isolation. As I took those first few steps into the wild, I realized that I finally truly felt alive.

As the mountains were drawing closer, I noticed their incredible beauty. They were a little intimidating but beautiful. The highway I was on had become steep and twisted, so I was tiring quickly. I came upon an outdoor center. They offered float trips and other similar adventures to travelers. I ventured inside and found a topographical map of the area. The clerk asked me where I was headed, and I said casually, "Just out to wander for a while". She smiled and said "Very cool, be careful." I thanked her and walked outside. At a bend in the road ahead, there was a hill to the right. I could see a clearing through the trees. I hiked up the hill and made my way through it. I will never forget that view. I sat there the rest of the afternoon, just staring up at the mountains, hoping for a safe but exciting journey.

Eventually, I left the road behind, following a decent-sized river upstream as it flowed down from the mountains. I'll never forget that day. It was perfect, sunny, and the air was amazingly clear and fresh. The sounds of the river rambling along soothed me and I traveled further and further into the wild. Although I was used to the weight of my pack by this point, I was about to discover the heaviest things I carried were my thoughts. Visions of my children crying careened about inside my head. The loop of my mother's cruel voice echoed as a relentless reminder of every failure. I wondered; would my steps now finally prove she was right?

It was already cooling off quite a bit at night, and I knew it wouldn't be long until winter fully arrived. Although I didn't have a tent, I was skillful in shelter building and had a quality sleeping bag, boots, and winter clothing. I immediately began searching for a good spot to set up camp. I was looking for something on the western slope of a valley, to help minimize the constant winds from that direction. I also needed a water source and a wooded area for trapping game.

I followed the river for probably a week, catching the occasional fish and finding lots of plants to eat near the water. Eventually, I found the area that would become my new home. It was a wooded area, tucked in near a bend in the river, and was everything I was seeking. I stopped for a minute to take in the amazing beauty that surrounded me. It was midday, and the sun was in full splendor. The tops of the valley were relatively high, which meant less time in the sun but being out of the wind was more important. I looked around in the woods and found a nice flat spot where the valley started to rise up away from the river. I stashed my pack there and hiked upriver for a while to make sure I was completely alone. I hadn't seen any signs of civilization in over a week except for the occasional plane overhead. I found nothing - no trails or roads; no people; nothing but me and the wild. It was almost perfect.

Crushing thoughts would come at times. Visions of my children crying because they didn't know why I had left them, where I had gone, or if I was alive or dead. It had been quite some time now and there was no escape from the torment inside my head. It devoured my spirit and all I could do was lay there, crying. I wanted to go back in an instant and unlive all the time I had been gone, just to see them and hold them, and to let them know they were loved.

But Lana was still in my head too. It was too risky. I was stuck with this agony, and I knew that nothing I did would take it away. I knew that I had failed them. I had failed everyone including myself. I decided the best thing I could do now was to stay alive. Stay out here long enough to get my head right, and maybe then I could return. I got up. I wiped away my tears and looked around. Wood. I needed to gather wood. I began.

That first evening I had dinner consisting of rice and Queen Anne's lace root. I made a simple lean-to with my tarps and tried to sleep. I barely slept at all. I was wrought with intrusive thoughts. I heard coyotes throughout the night, but I was already getting used to them by now. I knew I needed to start working on building a shelter, so I started to go over the plans I had written in my head, to distract me from everything else invading my mind. As I was reviewing every detail, the wind started to pick up. It wasn't cold, so that meant the possibility of a storm. I tightened everything down and waited it out. It rained relentlessly for what felt like hours. It was loud against my tarp. The wind was blowing the rain sideways into the opening. Eventually, the storm subsided, but I was soaked. As I lay there, shivering my way through the rest of the night, I anxiously awaited the morning light so I could begin work on my new temporary home.

17

SHELTER

Where thou art, that is home.

Emily Dickenson

    I don't know how long I slept, but I awoke just before dawn and the sky was clear. I nearly jumped up with sheer determination. Today was the day to start building my house. I had been working over the plans for it in my head for a very long time. In my mind, I had built it log by log hundreds of times. When you are walking along all by yourself, there is endless time to think about such things.

    The first thing to do was dig. I was going to build a pit house to help regulate temperature throughout the winter. I pulled out my camp shovel and got to work. Digging was tedious and hard, especially with such a short-handled shovel. I made steady progress though, and by mid-afternoon, had most of the two-foot-deep foundation dug and cleared out. By this time, I was hungry and decided to see if I could catch a fish for dinner. I hiked 200 yards to the bank of the river and cast my line. I had found a lot of worms while digging the foundation and was not going to let them go to waste. It wasn't too long before I caught a nice trout of about nine inches. I was overjoyed with my success. I headed back to camp, built a fire, and ate. After my feast, I dug a bit more, stopping periodically to witness everything around me. It was like a coin. One minute, I was on one side, on top of the world in a beautiful place, and then, in the next, I was on the other side, darkened with thoughts and devastation. I was never just okay or bored. My mind just kept jerking from one extreme to the other. My solution was to stay busy, and there was plenty to do.

    The next morning, I started on the walls. I used my saw to cut what seemed like an unfathomable number of medium-sized trees. I trimmed them and cut them to length. I then cut notches in the shorter ones, so the logs making up the long walls would sit in the notches and minimize gaps in the wall. This was similar to the way Lincoln Logs fit together. I managed to build the walls in one day and assemble them around the pit I had dug. The house itself would be about six feet wide by ten feet long. With the pit, it would be plenty deep enough to stand comfortably inside. I decided to stop for the day. I needed to be careful with my calorie expenditure. I set some snare traps along a game trail that ran through the forest to the north of my shelter. I wasn't feeling like fish, so I had oats.

That night, the rain came. I was dry under my tarp but was hoping to get my shelter completed soon. I hadn't seen any bears yet, but I knew they were around. The shelter would hopefully give me peace of mind. I would be in an enclosed structure versus lying out in the open like I was. It continued to rain all the next day, so I didn't make much progress on the shelter. I cut the door out of one of the ends and worked on cutting the logs into burnable-sized pieces for my fire pit. I spent the rest of the day sitting in my shelter, going over in my mind the exact way I wanted to construct the roof.

I checked my traps around dusk and nothing. I hadn't expended a lot of calories that day, so I wasn't tremendously hungry. I decided to conserve my supplies and just go without eating. I boiled some water and made pine needle tea. It felt good to have warmth in my belly, and I slept soundly with the rain falling on the tarp.

The next day dawned bright and crisp. I had another cup of tea and got to work on the roof. I framed it up rather quickly and cut beams for the rafters. After lashing them to the top post, I gathered evergreen boughs to place on the top to keep the rain out. It was starting to look like a small home, and I couldn't wait to move into it. I was getting hungry with all the day's activities and decided to check my traps in midafternoon. I was in luck. In the very last trap, there was a good-sized rabbit. I cleaned and skinned him away from camp, buried the innards, and hauled my prize back to camp. I remember that meal. It was so delicious and fulfilling. I ate everything. I devoured the heart, liver, and brain along with the body. Before going to bed, I decided that with my luck and a wonderful dinner, I would be ready to start building the chimney tomorrow. That meant a tremendous number of trips hauling rocks back from near the river. It had to be done, and I was motivated to finish and move in. I was so close!

I awoke the next day and had some pine needle tea to get me going. I wasn't feeling quite right, but I shrugged it off and headed down to the river to begin hauling the rocks for the chimney. I made about three or four trips and was looking for some good flat rocks when I heard a loud voice coming from back near my camp say "YOU'RE NEVER GOING TO SURVIVE THIS" I stood there frozen, not sure what to do. I never went anywhere without my big hunting knife, and I unlatched it and tried to see through the trees. My heart was racing and about to leap out of my chest. I was taking the first steps back when he shouted again "YOU'LL DIE OUT HERE!" I froze again, shaking with panic and barely able to breathe. After a couple of moments, I mustered up the courage to see what was going on. I pulled out my knife, holding it at my side, and started moving as quietly as I could towards my camp. The thoughts in my head were like ribbons flying around in a tornado. I couldn't settle on one before 20 others came whipping into my mind.

I was inside the tree line now and could see my camp in more detail. There didn't seem to be anybody around. I stopped near a big tree and was trying to think rationally about what to do next when suddenly, from the direction of the river where I had just come from, the man said, "YOU'RE SUCH A LOSER, IT WOULD BE BETTER IF YOU JUST DIED!" Now I was freaked out. Either this guy was some sort of ninja, or, as it was starting to dawn on me, I was hallucinating. After standing there shaking for several moments, I settled on the latter and put my knife away. "I HATE YOU!" echoed through the trees in the most horrible voice I had ever heard. I made my way back to camp and checked all around to make sure nobody was there. I was waiting until my cabin was done to move in, but I thought today was an exception. I moved my sleeping bag in there and lay down. The day was indeed becoming unbearable. I was in a constant state of panic and dread. The relentless barrage of demeaning comments was beating me down in a way I had not experienced since the voice I heard before my suicide attempt. It was saying similar things, but it sounded different. Different enough that I was completely convinced there was an actual person in my camp shouting at me.

I have never wanted music so much in my entire life. I had been missing it since riding with Walter. It had always been such a salve for me. I tried to think about songs I knew on piano and guitar in as much detail as possible. I played them in my head as best I could until suddenly, the voice roared again,

"YOU'LL NEVER AMOUNT TO ANYTHING!"

"YOU ARE THE WORST FATHER EVER!"

It went on like this all day, inexorable as heavy surf beating down upon the rocks. Thankfully, around dusk, the voice got quieter, and the interruptions to the concert in my head got further apart. I fell asleep shortly after that and slept well. I was mentally exhausted from battling that voice all day. I ended up waking up in the middle of the night. I went out to the river so I could see the stars clearly and estimated it to be somewhere around three or four. I went back to camp and then decided to hike out and check my traps. They were all empty and still set. I didn't want to haul rocks in the dark, because the chances of falling and twisting an ankle or hitting my head were too high. I decided to stay around camp and cut the hole at the base of the wall for the fireplace. It was on the short wall opposite the door and was about three feet high. After this was done, I built a fire and heated some water for tea. I was hungry, and still shaken by the voice, but determined to keep my mind and hands busy.

I treated myself to a breakfast of oats and was ready to go at first light. I spent the rest of the day hauling rocks back to the cabin, stopping to arrange them in a U shape out from the wall. By late afternoon, I was hungry, so I decided to check the traps. Empty. I grabbed my fishing gear and headed down to the river. I could see the fish swimming, but none took my bait. With the absence of luck this time, I suddenly got the idea to make a fishing spear. I was hoping it would work because when winter settled in, I wouldn't have access to worms any longer.

I was famished from hauling rocks all day, so I ate a modest amount of rice and lost count of how many cups of pine needle tea I had that night. Pine needle tea was more than just a warm comfort, it provided vitamin C in my diet. This was important to prevent the onset of scurvy. The fireplace was more than halfway finished. I found a good branch for a spear and began shaping it and working on the tips while sitting by the fire. Eventually, I was tired and headed to bed.

The next day, I was plagued by guilt and dread over leaving my family. I was struggling with intense negative thoughts and was on the verge of quitting and heading out of there. I knew I wasn't even close to ready, so I stayed. I was in torment all the time. I couldn't go back to where I was, and it was an endless wilderness in every direction. My only hope was that eventually the voices and guilt would diminish and I could carry on. I had no plan other than what was in front of me. In its own way, that was empowering.

It was early and I was thinking about what to eat. I was perpetually hungry. I was burning more calories than I was taking in by a long shot, and my pants were getting looser and looser. I didn't recognize my hands. They were thin and bony, and the veins were more pronounced than usual. I was starting to feel overwhelmed with despair again when I heard an animal. It was wailing and thrashing about in the brush. It was coming from the area near my traps. A rush of adrenaline made me almost forget about everything else. I made my way over there, and a beautiful snowshoe hare was caught by his front leg in one of my snares. That's why there was so much noise. Usually, the snare went around their neck, and it was over quickly and silently. This meant I was going to have to kill him on my own. I didn't think about it too much because I was so hungry, but I did debate for a while on how to do it. Eventually, I decided to hold him by the head and break his neck. I hope that it was merciful and painless.

    I reset my trap, cleaned him, and went back to camp. I had been thinking about things to keep me busy once the cabin was built that didn't involve burning a lot of calories. One of the things I decided to do was save the rabbit skins, brain tan them, and make moccasins and maybe a scarf. I ate well, saved the brain, secured everything at camp, and set out with a full belly to finish gathering and assembling the fireplace.

    I finished with the rock portion of the fireplace around noon and set out to gather mud and moss to plug all the cracks. I caught a small fish later that afternoon and had it with some watercress that I had gathered.

    I woke up the next day feeling a little off. Not quite sure how to describe this feeling, just that something wasn't right. I was having trouble keeping my thoughts on track as I worked on the door to the shelter. I was almost finished when Claire showed up. She scared me, standing just inside the tree line to the north of the shelter. I took a break and worked on some breathing exercises and tried to meditate to calm my mind. It was impossible to close my eyes because I was afraid she would sneak up on me. I had that prevailing fear that my hallucinations would become physical and visceral, digging their teeth into me while I slept or turned away. It's hard to describe what that feeling is like. My mind tells me she's there, I can see her, but rationally I know that she's not. Wrestling with this dual reality is difficult. After about 30 minutes of trying to calm myself unsuccessfully, I decided to busy myself by finishing the door. It didn't take very long. It consisted of a basic rectangle of branches, with two long ones, then lashed together with a paracord. The paracord took the longest, as I kept looking up to see where she was. Eventually, I fell into a rhythm and then I was done. I went to check my traps. Nothing. I decided to try and fish for a while but was unsuccessful. Claire was there for all of it, standing about 20 feet away, talking nonstop, although there was no sound. I resorted to rice and some wild onions that I had found a few days prior.

    I decided to sleep in the shelter that night. I was hoping that Claire wouldn't follow me in there. As I sat by the fire trying to focus on the stars and not Claire, I thought about my children. I knew that nobody knew where I was, nor if I was alive or dead. I felt monumental guilt, shame, and overwhelming sadness. It hit me hard all of a sudden and I wept deeply for quite some time. Eventually, I gathered myself, moved one of the larger pieces of wood to the fireplace in the shelter, and put out the outside fire. I was emotionally and mentally exhausted. Having Claire there all day was taxing on my mind and spirit. I closed the door, put on some extra wood, and spent my first night in my new home. Claire did not follow me in there. That was truly wonderful and such a relief. In my mind though, she was lurking just outside. I did eventually fall asleep, and despite not knowing where I was when I first woke up, I slept well.

Life in the wild continued much as it had for well after the first snow. My cabin was warm, and I missed my children desperately, but I was also really worried about going back to my children with the mental state I was in. I was having subtle symptoms daily now and had started to go a little mad wondering if everything I heard and saw was real. Even the birds seemed to be spying on me. I kept thinking they were high-tech drones of some sort. I spent a lot of time in my cabin. I only went out for food, water, or gathering wood. As it got colder, I spent more and more time out gathering wood.

There's a song by Tom Petty in which he laments, "Some days are diamonds, some days are rocks." I've certainly had my share of rocks, but what I discovered was that you will be able to do more with a rock than you ever will a diamond. The Great Wall of China was built with rocks. It reminds me of a haiku that I composed while hiking, which I committed to memory:

> Small stone in my shoe.
>
> I leave it there forever.
>
> Present, with each step.

18

LEAVING HOME, AGAIN

*In the midst of movement and chaos,
keep the stillness inside of you.*

Deepak Chopra

A few weeks after the first snow, I stopped getting rabbits in my traps. I still had fish, but the rabbits seemed to have been trapped out. I had a decision to make, could I survive the next few months on fish? If not, I was going to have to pack up and move to a new trapping area. This meant building a new shelter in the dead of winter. The only other option was to hike way further up towards the ridge to trap, which meant more calories expended. I wasn't sure what to do.

One night, I had a particularly bad barrage of nightmares about my mother. She was hiding behind trees and yelling insults at me. Her words were little bits of fire that would fly out into the open and burn if they hit me. She seemed to be everywhere, coming out from behind trees all around. I awoke quite shaken and demoralized. I went for a short walk, trying to decide what to do. I decided that occupying my mind would be a good thing for me. I spent the first few hours looking at my maps. I decided to head north along the river and deeper into the Sawtooth Wilderness. I knew I needed to go at least five miles away to be able to set new traps. However long it took, I would keep going until I found a perfect place. I began the process of gathering all my things back into my pack.

By studying the map, I realized I could cut across through the woods away from the river and the terrain would be a lot less daunting. I could then rejoin the river when it bent back to the northwest. I wasn't sure what I was going to find, so I took a moment to admire my shelter and say goodbye to what had been home for what seemed like a very long time. Everything slows down in the wild. Days seem to linger on much longer than normal, and nights often seem to last for a year. Even though it had only been a few months, it felt like I had been in that shelter for years.

19

DOWN

What does not kill me makes me stronger.

Fredrich Nietzsche

There were about eight inches of fresh snow from the night before. The snow was glistening in the light of the morning as if each snowflake was shimmering to guide my way. It made the trek seem very serene and scenic. It was a bright sunny day and for a change, I was feeling pretty good and free of symptoms. I trudged through the woods, being careful and measured with my steps. I didn't want to sprain an ankle with all the unseen brush on the forest floor beneath me. After what seemed like about an hour, I came to a clearing. I started across and was about halfway to the tree line on the other side when suddenly I heard a loud resounding ricochet that seemed to travel right out from beneath me. I suddenly realized I was standing on ice!

I took a few sharp but measured breaths of the cold air. Another thunderous crack shattered the silence around me. I immediately unbuckled the chest and waist straps of my pack and was about to take it off and lay flat, when the ground beneath me gave way and I abruptly fell through the ice. I broke through with my 50-pound pack still on. I swear my heart stopped from the shock. I was trying hard not to panic. The staggering jolt of the freezing water tore into my body like sharp blades of glass. My feet weren't touching the bottom. I tried to take a deep breath but only managed a shuddering gasp. The icy water gripped me like a full-body vice. I managed to get out of my pack and push it up onto the ice. That pack was my life. It had in it everything I needed to survive. I knew that if I lost it, I would be as good as dead. I took a few deep breaths, making sure to keep my limbs moving as much as possible.

I pushed my pack forward on the ice and while kicking with my legs, pulled myself up little by little using my pack as a counterweight. Time seemed to stop and what was probably only a minute or two seemed like forever. My legs were going numb, and I was tiring incredibly quickly. I could feel my heart racing against my ribs at a frenetic pace. I had to keep going. I felt very heavy with my winter clothes weighing me down. I had run marathons, but this was far more excruciating. I was completely exhausted, struggling to even breathe or kick.

Finally, I was out.

I slowly crawled away from the hole in the ice, shivering so hard I thought I was going to break my back. When I was far enough away, I mustered up what little strength I had left to stand. I carried my pack in front of me and painfully ran with scattered steps to the shore.

The first thing I did was remove my clothing. I knew that save for a pure wool sweater (which I didn't have) the clothing would only insulate the cold against my skin. Next, I pulled out my fire bundle. I always carried kindling and shredded cedar bark or some other tinder in a dry bag at the top of my pack for an emergency fire. Within a moment, I had it going. I stayed with it briefly but managed to tear myself away from it to gather larger pieces of wood.

My ears were ringing loudly. I found out later it was due to the blood pressure change caused by the constriction of all but the major blood vessels. Eventually, I had a roaring fire and was standing there in my underwear and boots. This was near-death experience number one. I very easily could have drowned, lost all my gear, or frozen to death.

Falling through the ice that day has come to symbolize a triumph of the spirit, of my spirit. Terrible things may happen, such as being locked in a closet or awakening to a world where reality is skewed, altered, dangerous, or scary. I've been through so much, but I never once stopped pulling myself back up onto the ice. I could have very easily taken the victim's path. Blaming everything in my life on the actions and words of others. I never have. I see it this way: Yes, I had a difficult childhood and an equally difficult adult life. I could go on using that as the reason for every bad behavior I commit, or I could rise above it, learn from it, and create the next best version of myself in each new moment.

This is one of the main principles I want to convey through this book. Many of us go through horrible things, but those of us who can close the door to the past, pull ourselves up, and rise to the best of our days are the true victors. That is the only way we can truly defeat our demons or the people in our past. If we live our lives constantly reacting to things out of fear, or blaming our bad behavior on our past, then we are still being tormented by whatever happened. In that, they still have power over us. I was, and still am determined not to let my past with my mother dictate my current behavior. It took a lot of work to get here, but as I sit writing this, I have truly emerged from the rubble and stand empowered and victorious in the best of my days. I still have triggers, but I now have the mental acuity and skill to react out of love in each situation. We can all do this. You don't have to go into the wilderness to do it either. My transformation didn't truly take place until ten years after my backpacking trip was over.

Eventually, I made my way down through the woods and rejoined the river going north. I stopped to fish, caught one, and ate it right on the bank of the river. It was in these quiet peaceful times, with the beauty of the world all around me, that my mother's voice would come rattling around in my mind like a rock in a dryer - not a hallucination, just thought memories pushing through. *'What is everybody thinking about you, running away like this? Our family is embarrassed.'*

I drove them away, focusing on the sun on my face and the food in my belly. Sometimes they would still creep in. I would turn to music, playing along to the song in my head. In my mind, I must have composed a thousand masterpieces in the wilderness. They are all gone now, left to blow around in the leaves, but they kept me alive.

20

A NEW FACE

Perspective changes everything, and perspective is always changing.

Todd Arkyn Crush

    I hiked further up the river and found a place to camp for the night. I was hoping the next day I would find a good spot to build a new shelter. It was a peaceful night, but I didn't sleep very well. With only a tarp and my sleeping bag, the frigid winter temperature sent chills through my bones. The icy dark was not the only thing keeping me awake. Constant disturbing thoughts wandered through my mind. What did my kids think happened to me? Were they lying in bed at night wondering, "Is he dead?" "Is he coming back?" "Where did he go?" or the one question that disturbed me the most, "WHY did he leave us?"

    I couldn't go back. I refused to endanger them in any way. I did not intend to live my life in an institution pumped full of drugs either. I did miss them terribly and I agonized heavily over what they were enduring at my expense.

    The next day I awoke with murmurs. To me, they always sound like someone talking a small distance away. I can never quite figure out where they are coming from and can't discern what they are saying. While it is one of my lesser hallucinations, they are still quite alarming. In the wilderness, with the trees and ridges all around, they are particularly unnerving. My brain is telling me there are people near me talking. I can't see them, but I can hear them. I can't make out the words, but I feel certain they are talking about me. I can't pinpoint where they are. What I am hearing could be real people. They might be coming to get me. Ugh.

    I packed up amidst all of this, determined to stay busy. A couple of miles up, I found a spot nearly identical to the one where I had previously built my first cabin. I called out "Anybody here?!?!!?!" Nobody answered. The murmurs continued to rattle away, but by this time, I had surmised they didn't count. I smiled at the thought of this. I dropped my pack, took my water bottle and knife, and decided to have a good look around.

It was a nice area and was maybe even a little nicer than the previous camp. There were several active game trails back by the ridge, all with fresh scat and tracks. There was a natural eddy in the stream which would lend itself greatly to spearing fish. The best way to distract myself from the murmurs was to stay busy, so I immediately got to work. I set a few snares back near the ridge and worked on constructing a cooking fire pit. It was a cold night and I knew I needed to get started on the shelter the next day.

I built the second cabin almost identical to the first one. The process went relatively well and within a few days, my new home was built. I would spend the duration of the Idaho winter in this humble place. I found another trapping area just an easy hike only a half hour away and the fishing was also good there. Although it was a decent location for rabbits and fish, I often had daily symptoms of anxiety and paranoia. At times, the insurmountable grief and regret I felt about leaving my children was almost unbearable. Yet I pressed on. Something inside of me was telling me that this had to be done. I didn't know why at the time, but years later the value of this time would be revealed.

There were several stints throughout the rest of that winter that I went without food for five, seven, and once eleven days. The lack of nourishment, in conjunction with the isolation I was feeling, had me confused and I was unable to think clearly. I realized at one point that it had been a long time since I had seen my own reflection. I went down to the water to wash up and see if I could catch a glimpse, but the water was flowing too swiftly around in the stream. I wondered how long it had been. It must have been way back at the truck stop before I headed out here. That was a long time ago. I wondered what I looked like.

Eventually, I could see the first signs of spring and felt a great sense of joy and pride. I had made it through winter without a tent! As the snow melted, and the air warmed, I had more and more rabbits in my snares. Just as with the earth, I felt rejuvenated. One morning, I walked down to the stream to wash up. I stripped down to undies and boots and started cleaning myself.

Suddenly, I heard a rustle behind me on the bank. I turned slowly to look. Standing there at the water's edge was a large black bear staring at me. I was just about to stand and yell to scare it away when I heard another rustle, this time from down the swell in the river to my left. Two small cubs had come out of the underbrush and were rolling around near the water. I was between the mother and her cubs.

My heart rate skyrocketed. The mother's eyes were locked on mine. I carefully backed my way through the creek to the opposite side and walked slowly away until I wasn't between them anymore. She watched me the entire time. Eventually, she must have decided I wasn't a threat and went over to her cubs and nudged them apart. They carried on together down the bank and around the bend.

The isolation, voices, and periodic lack of food were starting to wear me down. I had lost a lot of weight. The mental anguish of losing my children plagued me the most. The voices and hallucinations were growing in frequency and made daily life very difficult. I desperately missed music. I didn't realize until that time how soothing music was when voices were rambling away in my mind. I would have done almost anything for a player and set of headphones during those days. However, I learned early on in this journey, that acceptance is key. I had to accept and be grateful for what I did have and realize that there were things that I didn't. All the wishes in the world weren't going to manifest a pair of headphones.

As I started planning to break camp and figure out which direction to head next, I wondered what would become of me. I was terrified of re-entering society because of everything I was experiencing. I was sure if anyone found out, they would put me in an institution for the rest of my life. I knew I couldn't hold down a job. Relationships were out of the question. I didn't know how long I could stay out here. Eventually, my gear and my body would start breaking down. I had decided this would be my last time choosing to survive winter in the north. I had had enough of the dreadful winters growing up in Wisconsin. I was proud that I had done it here in Idaho. It surely wasn't without trial and tribulation. I looked at the cabin that I had built, thought about the horrible endless nights in there with voices in the dark, and wondered who would find it next.

With the thaw in full force, I broke camp and headed north along the river. The wilderness seemed endless. I carried on for several days and nights (I often lost track of the days). Eventually, I came to a road. I was surprised at how effortless it was to hike on the smooth surface. It had been many months since my boots had touched anything other than backwoods terrain.

After a few weeks, I was in Western Montana sitting in front of a gas station in a little town called Dillon. When I went in to use the bathroom, there was a greasy blurry mirror above the sink. It was one of those metal mirrors that makes everything seem not just blurry, but as if it's subtly in motion. I was shocked at the person I saw. I didn't recognize myself at all. It had been months since I had seen my own reflection. In modern society, we don't realize it, but we see ourselves all the time. We look in the mirror when we wash our hands, brush our teeth, or when we are putting makeup on our faces. The extended absence from glancing in a mirror was very unsettling to me.

My face was thin and gaunt. My cheekbones stuck out above my long and unruly beard. My lips seemed thin and pulled back over my teeth. There were several deep lines in my face around my eyes that weren't there a year ago. It was truly shocking to see that version of me. I forced a smile, but it appeared across my face more like a wince. I was here, I was alive, but the long months of survival had taken its toll and the harshness of it was staring back at me.

21

AMONG THE HORSES

Let the beauty of what you love be what you do.

Rumi

I eventually went back outside. I was drinking water and looking around at the quiet mountain town. A beat-up Hummer pulled up and a man got out. He smiled and went into the station. After a few minutes, he came out with two coffees and handed me one. I thanked him and he asked where I was from. I told him Michigan and proceeded to tell him one of the back stories I had created. In this one, my wife and I were avid hikers. She died in an accident, and I set out to hike the country in her honor. He said that was nice and would love to hear some stories about my travels. He told me his name was Brad and we talked for a while. He told me he owned a horse ranch and that his son had recently broken his leg playing football and was unable to help. He asked if I would be interested in helping for a fair wage plus room and board. I needed new boots and a tent really would be nice, so I agreed.

At this point, he put his hand on my shoulder. I jumped. A shadow of alarm cast across his face. I apologized and explained that it had been quite some time since I had any physical contact. He nodded in a way that made me feel better about the whole thing. The next thing I knew I was riding in the Hummer on the highway. I can't explain the anxiety that was welling up inside of me. Not because of Brad's driving, but from the sheer speed at which I was travelling. It had been almost a year since I had been in a vehicle and the whole thing had me unsettled.

Eventually, we arrived at his ranch and Brad showed me around. I had a nice room upstairs and I got to meet his wife and son. That night we had a nice dinner, but it was a bit overwhelming for me. I was only used to eating very small portions so I couldn't eat very much, but I savored every single bite. I went to bed early but found myself tossing and turning. I was used to sleeping outside on the ground. The bed was much too soft. After a while, I pulled the blanket onto the floor and slept there. It was a good night's sleep. I awoke early in the dark to find Claire standing a few feet from me. It really scared me, and I almost cried out. I dressed quickly and turned on the light and my clock radio. The music helped and I did some deep breathing to further settle me down. Dawn came with her still there. Suddenly there was a quiet knock at the door, and I opened it to find Brad, ready to go.

"Good you're dressed, come down and have some breakfast and I will show you some things to get started on today."

"Sure thing!" I swallowed hard, looked back briefly at Claire, and headed downstairs. It was hard eating with her standing there, hiding my symptoms all over again. I missed the woods, but at the same time was grateful to be around good people.

I spent the summer there, leading the horses up to high pasture and watching over them. I was given other tasks as well and certainly enjoyed my time. The regular food and shelter were comforting, although dealing with hallucinations was difficult with everyone around. I had periods of time alone, too. My favorite was being in the pasture all alone with the horses. I would sit next to a rifle and watch for coyotes. Brad instructed me that I didn't have to shoot the coyote, just fire the gun in the air. He had conditioned the horses not to bolt when they heard the shot. Thankfully, I never had to use the gun. Although it was some of my most memorable times, being in the pasture was not without tribulation.

One day, early in the morning, I was having coffee and watching the horses in the pasture. I had a serene and peaceful feeling inside. Suddenly, a man appeared across the meadow holding a rifle. He wasn't aiming it at me, but he just stood there with it on his shoulder. He was big and I was rattled. I managed a wave, but he just switched the rifle from one shoulder to the other. Panic rose in me steadily and thick like sauce just starting to boil. I looked briefly at the rifle leaning against the tree to my right, and when I looked back, he was walking slowly towards me.

Now the panic was like a raging water boiling over. I tried to talk myself down. 'Maybe he's one of Brad's friends...' 'Maybe I'm in the wrong place and he's pissed...' I was doing a very poor job of trying to calm myself. I looked again at my rifle, and when I looked back up, he was gone. I was completely fooled again. I totally thought he was real. I was once again reminded of the terrifying truth that my life would be like this for the rest of my days. I would have to live never really knowing what was real and what was in my head. It's a maddening way to exist.

By August, I was starting to get antsy and knew I needed to head south before winter. I had saved up enough money to get new boots, a tent, and a nice water purifier. I was ready to be out there again. I was grateful for the extra money but knew it was time to go. After a nice dinner and a wholesome goodbye, I packed up and headed out the next morning at dawn. This time, I went southwest.

22

THE SCORPION

*One does not find enlightenment by imagining figures of light,
but by making the darkness conscious.*

Carl Jung

At some point in my journey southwest, I decided I wanted to hike the entirety of Death Valley. After a relaxing winter in Northern California, I headed towards the valley. I arrived with a bag of rice, and a few other staples, and was pretty sure I could do it. I ventured out sometime in May, which meant 100 degrees or so during the day, and 60 degrees at night. This temperature change was critical to my survival. My most valuable piece of gear was a three-foot square section of clear plastic. I would use this to make a solar still every night and collect the condensation each morning. It wasn't much, but it would keep me alive.

At roughly 140 miles long, I calculated if I hiked ten miles a day, I would be able to make it all the way through in two weeks. It was a rough plan, but it was a plan. Unfortunately, things did not go according to plan. After a few days, I was growing increasingly weak. Dry rice and jerky were keeping me moderately fueled, but I did not have a lot of water. I came across a small campground, but it was closed, and the water was shut off. I was demoralized, but I kept going. I'm not sure how far in I was but I estimate I must have been about halfway. I was sleeping in my bag out in the open without a tent.

Half asleep and extremely thirsty, I slowly turned to reach for my water bottle. Suddenly I felt an excruciating stabbing pain in my left bicep. I tore open my sleeping bag to discover a rather large bark scorpion lodged in my armpit. He immediately started to crawl away, so I quickly grabbed my knife and stabbed him into the ground.

I fought the urge to panic. I took several deep breaths. I knew I needed to slow my heart rate, which would decelerate the spread of the venom. I also grabbed a bandana and made a tourniquet above the sting. Thankfully, I had been using several for sunscreen and had one handy. With one last deep breath, I reluctantly ate the scorpion raw. I had read about a Native American tracker who said that most venomous creatures contain an anecdote to their own venom. The secret was you had to eat them raw. I didn't have time to wonder if what I had read was true, so I cut off the stinger and wolfed it down.

It was absolutely deplorable and probably the most horrible thing I had ever had in my mouth. I had eaten spiders, bugs, and other vile creatures, but this was by far the worst. Despite my quick reaction, within 30 minutes, I was starting to feel increasingly ill. Since I was wide out in the open, I had previously set up my tent and put a tarp off to the side of it. This allowed me to lay in the open next to my tent and be in the shade. I was evaluating my water situation (about half a cup) when I started vomiting. I was already parched and sunbaked from days in the desert and knew this would further exacerbate my dehydration. Despite my situation, I was trying to be conservative and took the smallest of sips. I nibbled on dry rice for strength and hoped it would calm my stomach. After about an hour, I was having involuntary convulsions and my fever had spiked.

Eventually, I started losing consciousness. What seemed like seconds were most likely hours, possibly days, and vice versa. I would close my eyes in the searing noonday sun only to open them a second later and it was the middle of the night. In those moments between wakefulness and unconsciousness, I contemplated my death. Fading thoughts would drift in and out of my mind like waves washing on the shore. Who would find me out here? Would there be enough left of me to tell who I was? Should I carve a message in my arm for my kids? What should I say? I had lucid images of eventually being found, but all that was left were bones. There were some lingering notions of sinew or tendon, but most of what had made me me had long been taken away. In all my life, what had I added up to? This thought lingered in the trenches of despair in my mind.

Darkness is all around us, lurking around every corner. In every new moment, there is an option for the universe to sweep in and whisk life away. As quick as a final sharp breath, drawn in through clenched teeth, we are gone. Lifetimes passed before me as I lay there minute by minute, one breath at a time. As I lay there under the desert sky, the hallucinations came, vast star landscapes and diaphanous planets. Distances between myself and everyone I had ever known grew very short, and then very long. My children cried, I cried, my world disappeared and came back again. I was in and out of consciousness for several days and nights. As the fever from the venom raged within me, my thoughts rumbled away like the lowest notes on a piano, dissonant and callous, indifferent like impending thunder.

I turned inward.

Something in me, deep down, knew that I would see another day, and then another. Many years later I told these stories to a close friend. Her comment was succinct and poignant. "Wow, someone really wants you to be here." Around that same time, a therapist would ask me if my backpacking trip was a veiled suicide attempt. I wasn't sure then, but now as I look back, I think it might have been.

There was the God my parents tried to push upon me, one that I never believed in. It all seemed so far-fetched and I knew too much about science to take the Bible as truth. Yet, as I oscillated in and out of consciousness, I knew there was something else out there - out there in the desert where I lay dying - something that connects us all in a way that we don't need words to understand.

There is a presence in all of us that reveals something behind it all. It doesn't need a name, or a book, or a church. Its place is between everything that is. Even though where I was physically was akin to being on the surface of the moon, I certainly did not feel alone. My children were with me. Whatever that 'something' is, it was with me too.

I was too weak to dig a hole for my solar still, so my water quickly ran dry. I was reduced to drinking my own urine. When I look back and remember moments like these, I must question whether this was an unconscious suicide attempt. I certainly did everything I could to stay alive.

Eventually, I started to feel better. I dug my hole for my still, and lingered for a few days, completely resting and hydrating. I eventually hiked south and completed my trek of Death Valley. I immediately found the nearest town and used some of my money from the ranch to find a dingy hotel room. I remember drinking water for what felt like hours. All I could do was lay on the bed with the AC on full blast. I was too exhausted and traumatized to do much else. I turned on the TV, but the invasive sounds and mindless chatter were too much. I finally just lay there in silence, resting and thinking about what to do next.

23

VISITATIONS

Wilderness is not a luxury but a necessity of the human spirit.

Edward Abbey

    I spent the next several months in areas of California, Nevada, and Arizona. My hallucinations were ever present and continuously tormented me along with thoughts and guilt about my children. I had been gone for so long that I honestly had no idea what month it was.

    I had a pleasant experience in Nevada. I was sitting out in the desert on a large rock outcropping. I could not see much of anything in any direction. I was watching two vultures circling above, thinking 'Going to have to wait awhile fellas, I'm not dead yet...' As I casually looked to my right, the shadows of the vultures came together and formed a turtle, slowly drifting across the sand. In that moment I felt the nuances of the universe urging me on. I always carried a needle, thread, and India ink in my pack. I immediately pulled them out and tattooed the image of the turtle on my left calf while sitting there on the rock. Every time I look at it, I am reminded to keep going, to keep pushing, to carry on, and trust the process.

    Later, on my way east across Nevada, I developed a bad toothache in my lower right molar. I had no painkillers, and there were no willow trees nearby. Earlier in my trip, I had used the bark to make tea as a natural pain relief. I struggled for two days. Eventually, the pain became unbearable. I sterilized my knife and found a fist-sized rock. I lodged the tip of the blade as deep as I could along the gum line of the afflicted tooth and tapped my knife with the rock. Eventually, about 30 horrific minutes later, the tooth was out. I was relieved, but also worried about infection. I rinsed my mouth repeatedly and decided not to eat for a few days.

    I stumbled into St. George, Utah, and hiked south along the Virgin River Gorge. It was tough terrain, wrought with steep cliffs, several crossings, and loose ground. I was at the top of a ridge when suddenly the ground gave out below me. My pack and I went tumbling down a steep ravine. When I landed, my head slammed into a jagged rock. It knocked me out cold. When I came to, I had a large cut above my left eye that was bleeding profusely. I could not get it to stop. I tried to close it with tape, but it was too big and there was too much blood. I had purchased a small signal mirror a month or so prior, and with that mirror, my needle, and some fishing line, I stitched up my head. Luckily, I had some rubbing alcohol wipes that I had used to sterilize my instruments, so once I was done, I used them to clean the cut. I was worried about getting an infection, but thankfully I did not. I still have a small scar there, but it's barely visible unless you look closely. I guess I did a pretty good job considering blood was running down into my eye and the tools I had available were not intended for that purpose.

After leaving Utah, I crossed over into Colorado. I hiked around and found my way to the top of many mountains. I remember one in particular. I think it was Mt. Evans, but I can't be sure. At the time, I was manic and in psychosis. When I reached the top, I decided to camp up there. Camping was not allowed, but by this time, I had become quite an expert at stealth camping.

I had a decent night's sleep. When I woke, it was bright, cloudless, and sunny. I gathered my things and started down the trail toward the bottom. As I descended, the clouds thickened, and it was foggy. As I kept going, the fog was so dense it started to mist. I eventually arrived at a place where I could see through the trees. My head was level with the bottom of the clouds, and it was raining. It was truly a remarkable experience. For the first time since the hotel after Death Valley, I realized I had the power to control my environment. I turned around and hiked back up into the light of the sunshine for the rest of the day and night.

24

A CHANCE OF CLOUDS

*Travel, in the younger sort, is a part of education;
in the elder, a part of experience.*

Francis Bacon

Winter came and went in the desert Southwest. By this time, I had completely lost track of the months. I was wandering around Arizona when I found myself on the Hopi Indian Reservation. I went into a small general store and purchased a coffee. There was a porch out front, and I sat in one of the well-worn chairs to relax. It was mid-morning and was already getting quite warm. An elderly man came up and sat in a chair about seven feet from me. I glanced over at him, taking in his worn-in look and wrinkled face etched with decades of character and story. His face was ancient and weathered like pottery left in the desert sun for eons. He glanced at me, smiled, and said, "Where have you been?"

This opened a well of stories for me. I had not talked to anyone for quite some time, and although I was normally reticent, it all came pouring out like water. At some point, I realized I had been rambling on for a long time, and I stopped, smiling somewhat sheepishly. He smiled, and said, "That's a wonderful journey. I would love to hear more. You can call me Laughing Cloud."

I knew at that moment, the memory of him would be etched in my soul for the rest of my life. We talked for quite a while about many topics. He talked about the ancient ones and things he had witnessed over his long lifetime. I have always been interested in history, so it was fascinating to get his take on WWII, the moon landing, and the emergence of computers.

As it was, Laughing Cloud didn't have much in the way of technology. He lived with his wife, Etta, who was equally storied and wise, and his two grandsons, Pau, 11, and Jarreth, 9. They all lived in a modest one-room house on the edge of town. It was an old adobe structure decorated with various wood carvings and numerous cacti. Built into one wall was a large hearth. When we arrived, Etta was making bread. It smelled amazing. He introduced me, but everyone kind of carried on with what they were doing. Etta tended to her bread and the boys were watching some Western movie on a small TV in the corner. There wasn't much - a table and chairs, two queen beds, and a tall armoire in the corner, with clothes and blankets spilling out. There was also an old refrigerator. It was one of those models from the 50s with a big chrome handle and accents that made me think of an old Buick.

Laughing Cloud did not hesitate to ask me to help. I was more than happy to, so before long I was out back pumping water out of the well into buckets. When I returned to the house, the boys were roughhousing and nearly knocked one of the buckets from my hand.

"Time to run!!" Laughing Cloud said sternly and on point. The boys froze, lined up side by side, and he took a cup and filled it with water. The boys each took a sizeable drink but did not swallow. They held it in their mouth. After a brief pause, Laughing Cloud said, "Go!" The boys bolted out the door and I could see them running down the street towards the edge of town at a fast clip. While they were gone, Etta explained this was his way of dealing with their extra energy and rowdy behavior. When they got unruly, he would send them running to the end of town. When they returned, there was always a chore the loser of the race had to perform. They also had to spit out the water. If they swallowed it while running, they had to run again. I thought this was very wise. You might think it would have taught them to despise running, but they enjoyed it. The racing part was fun and they kept a tally of who won and who lost on the wall near their bed.

That evening we had a marvelous dinner. The fresh bread was especially wonderful. I slept on the floor under the window. I ended up staying for about a month with his family. Laughing Cloud and I spent a lot of time together. He tried to teach me how to whittle but I wasn't very good at it. The whole time I was there, I carved away at what was supposed to be an owl, but it was indistinguishable from an ear of corn when I left. He treasured it, nonetheless.

One day he shared with me various Native symbols that were passed down through the generations. One of my favorites was the Hopi symbol for the universe. I liked it and the magical story he told so much; I tattooed the symbol on my lower abdomen one evening just after the sun went down.

My favorite memories of Laughing Cloud were our trips on horseback out into the desert. We would pack up a few essential items and journey to the ruins of the ancient ones. I was taken by how, even as old as the ruins were, it seemed as if the Natives had been present there just the day before. There was pottery set out, waiting for food or water. A carved horse lay next to scraps of an old blanket. I felt honored to have gotten the chance to witness this sacred place. On the way there and back, he would tell stories, stories of the star children and the Hopi connection to the sky. I found his tales fascinating and it made me feel connected to something bigger than all of us. It reminded me of those spiritual moments during my near-death experience in Death Valley. The time I shared with Laughing Cloud is full of memories that will live in me forever.

After a while, I began to worry that my presence was a hindrance to the family. They had so little and sharing with me was certainly taking its toll. One morning, I gathered my things, and with a grateful heart, said my goodbyes and headed out. My time there was not without hallucinations. Claire was present a lot, and I almost told him several times but decided to keep it to myself. I was still too afraid to let anyone know what was happening to me. This fear would persist inside me for years to come. It wasn't until over a decade later when I met Lesli that everything began to change. I was finally ready to tell my story for the very first time.

25

UPON THESE WINGS

*I'll walk where my own nature would be leading:
It vexes me to choose another guide.*

Emily Brontë

After my stay on the Hopi reservation, I headed north back into Colorado for a bit. Colorado was difficult for me because everywhere I went, the trails were crowded with people and it was difficult for me to find solace alone. I decided to turn back west and cross back into Utah. Before long, I found myself in Canyonlands National Park. The rock formations were majestic, the sunsets were breathtaking, and it was easy to find a place to camp without people nearby. My plan was to enter The Maze, stay close to the river, and just wander around for a while. The Maze was the most remote, least accessible part of the area, so it was exactly what I wanted – a haven away from civilization where I could gather my thoughts.

I was still constantly haunted by hallucinations and voices and tormented with guilt. The canyons in this area are at least three to six hours by ATV from the ranger station. It is strongly recommended that hikers and visitors use a map to reach the area. I found out much later that GPS units frequently lead people astray, so a compass was questionable at best. There are no services, food, gas, or potable water sources in The Maze. I knew it was not much of a plan, but it was what I had at the moment.

Before long, I was completely lost. In a way, the feeling was somewhat liberating. I had fish, water, and shelter on my back. After what felt like a couple of weeks, I decided it was time to move on, so I set a goal to find my way out. The canyons turned, forked, and seemed impossibly endless. I wandered around for more than another week, before starting to become a little distraught. I was sitting on a large boulder and looked up to see a hawk circling above where the canyon split. He was flying over the gorge to the left. It felt like a sign, so I gathered my gear and followed him slowly in that direction. After a while the canyon split again, but this time the hawk was hovering to the right side. I followed again. This continued for what seemed like hours and on into the next day. Even as night fell, something was calling for me to keep going and adhere to his path. As I rounded one long turn down the next ravine, to my astonishment and delight, I found myself out of The Maze. I was in complete awe.

Again, I felt deeply connected to all that was around me. I resonated with the unity amongst living things in a way you can't get from reading books. You must become one with everything out there, living through it. I felt part of something much larger than I ever had before. I made camp and tattooed the hawk on my arm by the light of my fire that night.

I headed south again as winter was now quickly approaching. This time, I spent the cold months in New Mexico before deciding to head east during the spring. Somewhere near the Colorado and Kansas border, I developed another toothache. This time it was on the left side. The inevitable reality of what lay ahead was almost as piercing as the pain in my jaw. I rinsed as much as I could with water and was careful eating. It continued to get worse and worse. Eventually, I repeated the process with my knife and a rock, dislodging the molar after another grueling 30 minutes of agony. In the end, it was worth it. The pain subsided rather quickly. I continued my walk across Kansas. There were no scenic vistas, towering sandstone spires, or beautiful mountains to witness. Flat, windy, and lonely plains seemed to last for an eternity. I wanted to get to Georgia and the Appalachian Trail, so I had no choice but to walk this path.

It quickly became apparent that water would be scarce and camping would be difficult. There were very few wooded areas, so I often stopped early to huddle under a bridge or behind a hill. It was incredibly monotonous. It was the same landscape every single day. Nothing really to look at, just dry, dusty, windy, and hot. I got a short reprieve and found a large, wooded area with a nice river that flowed through. After rice and peanut butter for weeks, it was nice to have a few fish and rabbits. It was like a vacation from the dust of the plains. I felt like I hadn't seen trees for a year. I spent a couple of weeks and then was on my way out of there. I ventured down the road to the east but got to a place where the bridge was out, and the road just ended. It was kind of strange. I backtracked a bit, found a place to cross the river, and then continued east across the backcountry.

The next day I came to a large field, split up into 20-foot squares made with barbed wire. I had never seen anything like it. Almost as far as I could see to the left and right, was just a field of barbed wire squares. Nothing inside the squares, just an empty field. There were no signs, just a small round emblem on a post labeled 'Army Core of Engineers.' The barbed wire was the tightest I had ever encountered. It was so tense that I couldn't bend it to squeeze through. I had to decide – I either had to climb over each of the squares to get across or hike an unknown distance to make it all the way around.

I decided rather quickly to go over the fences and cross through the field. It was slow going and I was being extremely careful. After about four fences, I caught my right leg on the top of the wire. It split my leg wide open in two different places on the side of my knee. I sat in the center of the square, halfway across, holding a bandana over the wounds. Both cuts were too gaping to stitch, so I did the only thing I could. I built a small fire, heated my hunting knife until it was glowing hot, and cauterized the wounds. I cannot explain the pain. It was like a searing blade straight into my soul. I almost passed out from the pain. The most agonizing part of the experience was knowing there were two big gashes, so I had to do it twice. The second time was much harder than the first. The stabbing pain of the blistering knife was almost too much to bear. I sat for a while trying to ascertain what had just happened. With bandages on both throbbing wounds, I slowly staggered my way out of the bizarre area of land and moved onward to the east. I didn't know it yet, but my journey in the wild was coming to an end.

26

END OF THE LINE

Every day is a journey, and the journey itself is home.

Matsuo Basho

As I continued my way across Kansas, the lack of landscape and forest started to wear on me. I missed seeing the striking rock formations of the desert and the majestic comfort of the trees. The episodes of psychosis seemed to be taking permanent residence in my mind as their frequency began to increase.

The various backstories I had created began to manifest themselves deeper and deeper into my existence. They landed and became my truth for longer and longer periods, before leaping away only to be quickly replaced by another. I didn't just think about them, I became them. I lived every nuance of the lives I had created in my head. I saw Claire often, as well as other people out and about on the road. I thought they were real at first, but as I passed them, I would turn to look back and they had disappeared. In Kansas, there was nowhere for them to hide.

At some point, I veered off south and entered Oklahoma. I don't recall much about this part of my journey. I was so deeply imprisoned in altered states of reality, that the days were a blur. The epilogues in my head became so prominent that eventually, I couldn't find my way back to the truth. I have one faint memory of the last few days and nights before reaching Arkansas.

I must have been somewhere near the border and had taken quiet refuge behind a small gas station. A young woman suddenly appeared and was startled by my presence. She must have seen the hollow look in my eyes and gently asked if I was ok. I don't recall my answer, but in the space between reality and where the elaborate tales of my life had taken hold, I couldn't remember my own name.

I didn't know who I was.

Abruptly, a staggering wave of intense fear flooded over me. It was like being stranded in the middle of the ocean on a small raft in the dark. I had nothing to moor my psyche to. My self-identity was gone and I was left with a frightening feeling of emptiness. It was one of the scariest experiences in my entire life - more terrifying than falling through the ice, more jarring than the scorpion. I could do something about those, but with this, I was powerless. I had no past, no future, no present. There was not even an echo or whisper of the man I used to be.

Somehow, I managed to ask her where the nearest hospital was. With what little thread of lucid thought remained, a part of me knew my arduous five-year trip on foot had come to an end. She said I could head east and cross over a bridge; then told me to follow the signs. I vaguely remember the last few hours of my journey. I made it to Fort Smith, Arkansas, and went directly to the emergency room. I immediately told them I couldn't remember my name. They asked me several times about drugs, but I told them repeatedly I had not taken any.

Once they got my blood test results, they stopped asking, but I could tell they were alarmed at the state of my health. I was severely dehydrated and extremely malnourished. My emaciated face and rail-thin body were reminiscent of a concentration camp victim. They put me on two IVs right away and mentioned something about my potassium being gravely low. Before too long, the police showed up to ask me questions. They wanted to know where I had come from and probed me about people that I knew. I couldn't respond to them. I didn't have the answers. My mind was so clouded by the elaborate tales I had conjured that my confusion became my prominent voice. At times I would start to tell them one of the narratives I had created, and then quickly back away, saying something like 'Wait, that wasn't me'. They would look at each other, make a few notes, and then step outside to share their thoughts. After a while, it was apparent they were convinced that something else was going on.

Eventually, the hospital psychiatrist came to see me, and still not knowing my name, the interview was similar. The questions were a little more probative, asking about my childhood, if I had any children, pets, etc. I managed a few rough details, but it was not enough to figure out who I was or where I was from. I was in my own room at this point and terrified that I might never find out who I was. In the back of my mind, I was also scared I might find out the truth about myself and be horrified by the outcome.

When I was admitted, I weighed only 121 pounds. I was nearly six feet tall, so they knew I had been undernourished for quite some time. They were constantly bringing me food, but I could barely eat. My stomach was so used to eating very small portions it was very difficult to eat much of what they brought at first. Gradually, my appetite returned. Since my potassium levels were so dire, they had me constantly hooked up to an IV. I could not be admitted to the mental health facility until my levels came up. My fear of being locked away forever had somewhat subsided at this point. I still didn't know who I was or what my situation was. To myself and everyone else in the world at that time, I was known as John 31B. Until I figured out my past, I couldn't possibly have a future.

Eventually, I was moved to the mental health facility. Shortly after arriving, I was sitting at a table in the day room, when suddenly it all came flooding back. The reason I left, where I had been, and my fear of being in an institution forever. And here I was. The panic welled up in me like a shaken hornet's nest. I stood up and started pacing around, flipping my hands as if I were casting water off them. I don't remember what I said, but I was talking rapidly just under my breath; trying to calm down. It didn't work. The hysteria and fear got the best of me, and I broke for the door. It was locked securely, but I banged and pushed with all of my might.

By this time the nurse had alerted the staff, and two guys came, grabbing me by the arms roughly. I was yelling and flailing with everything I had. I was quickly strapped to a bed in a room, and given a shot in the arm something that almost instantly calmed me down. I still felt it though. The sheer horror wasn't as visible on the outside, but it was like I was screaming underwater.

At some point, strapped to that bed, I fell asleep. It's a petrified feeling to wake up in restraints. I felt trapped, and scared, and I was pretty sure I was going to be stuck there forever. I suddenly remembered the dark, ominous times in the closet as a child.

I was in that room for what felt like an eternity. Finally, just before I thought I was going to have an accident, they came in to let me go to the bathroom. They were talking to me in soothing voices, letting me know it was going to be okay. After I went to the bathroom, they took me to an office-type room. There was a desk and two chairs, but that was about it. Sharp objects and cords of any kind were kept out of places like this.

Finally, an older man with a gray beard and a medical file came in. He introduced himself and started asking me what had happened the day before. I finally just let it all out. I told him my fears of being locked up, my hallucinations, my fear of hurting others because of what Lana had done…all of it. He listened with a practiced ear, and when I was finished, smiled and leaned a little closer. "I can assure you, Todd, that you will not be here forever. Probably more like two weeks at the most. We will get you on medication to manage your symptoms, and there will be groups and therapy to deal with the trauma that you have endured."

I had never felt a bigger weight lifted off me in my entire life. I was a schizophrenic and someone else knew it. I felt like I had been holding my breath for over ten years. Part of me was still doubtful, but he seemed like a sincere and straightforward kind of person. All of a sudden, my paranoia kicked in. Maybe he was lying to me to keep me in line. Maybe the meds were a trick to keep me sick and give them a reason to keep me here. All of those notions subsided rather quickly, as thoughts of my kids came rushing in. I had to let them know that I was okay. I wanted to tell them everything, tell them why, and where I had been for so long. I went to the desk and said that I needed to make a call. It wasn't phone hours, but they made an exception because I had been missing and nobody knew where I was. I was hoping that my ex-wife's phone number was still working. It's the only one I had memorized. I dialed the number. It rang an agonizing four times and then I heard her voice.

"Hello?"

"It's me, I'm ok...."

"Oh....where are you?"

I explained where I was and started rambling and she abruptly cut me off.

"Listen, I'm glad you are okay, but you can't talk to the kids. I will let them know when I think they're ready, but you've done a lot of damage here. I hope that you get better soon. Please don't call again until we reach out to you..."

I sat in stunned silence for a few seconds. She was right. This was going to take a lot of time. I couldn't expect everyone to just pick up where we had all left off, after all, things were pretty dicey before I left as they were.

"I understand. Take care of yourself and the kids."

"Bye Todd."

"Goodbye."

No words could ever describe how much I appreciate everything my first wife did to care for our children. I know that my words will never be enough, but it needs to be said. As my life unraveled, she stepped in and completely took on raising our kids by herself. She did a remarkable job and deserves a tremendous amount of credit. All three of them turned out to be amazing people and always knew they were loved. Her compassion and understanding through all of this has been incredible. Until the revelations were presented in this book, neither she nor anyone else knew about my childhood or what was happening to me when the symptoms of schizophrenia hijacked my life. I am eternally grateful for everything she did.

Interlude...

My children have asked not to have a long-drawn-out apology and to move on. I have honored that. I will say, as I know it has been hard, that I wish I had been stronger for them when this all started. I wish I could have fought the way I am fighting now. I was not able to. I didn't have the courage or the will back then. I am grateful to have survived and elated to have this time with you now. I can't imagine what you went through. Leaving you the way that I did is one of my deepest regrets. I hope that through this book you realize that I was struggling so greatly, that my rational mind was not functioning. I left to protect you. In my mind, it was the only way to stay alive and keep you safe at the same time. I was terrified of the institution, but looking back now that probably would have been the better choice. In the least, you would have known that I was safe. I am so very proud of all of you, and it is my great joy to witness the paths your lives have taken.

I love you, Dad.

I slept well that night. One thing about the mental hospital, once everyone takes their medication, it's dead silent at night. They do come in periodically to check on you, but usually, it's not that intrusive. As the meds took hold, I settled into a routine and managed to make a few friends. One of them, Jeannie, and I spent most of our days together. We would sit in the day room, mocking the commercials, and talking under our breath about the staff and other patients. Thinking back, it sounds kind of pitiful, gossiping like that, but it kept us occupied. From the very beginning, she was like a sister to me. She was released about a week before me. Before she left, she slipped me a note with her phone number and told me to call her when I got out.

27

OUT THERE AGAIN

*He who learns but does not think, is lost!
He who thinks but does not learn is in great danger.*

Confucius

A week later, I was released from the ward and riding in a cab headed downtown. The support I got from the system amounted to one week of medication samples and a cab ride to the Salvation Army homeless shelter. That was it.

This level of support is not enough. A major reason today's mental health system is flawed is this fact. There is no long-term foundation of aid outside of the emergency mental wards. When you are released, you are on your own. If you don't have somewhere to go, you are homeless. It's a constant cycle of hospitalization, release, struggle, and rehospitalization. Sometimes, this pattern of events turns into tragedy, like with Lana.

I still had all my backpacking gear and the urge to disappear down the road to the east was very strong. I knew though that I needed to turn the page. I'd been down that path before. My cab arrived, and eventually, I stepped out at the homeless shelter. I immediately asked the lady at the front desk if there was a phone I could use. She directed me to a phone near the wall, with a big sign that said LOCAL CALLS ONLY. Thankfully, Jeannie's number was local and she answered right away. Within 20 minutes, I was in her car and we were heading to her duplex.

The spare bedroom was all set up for me and we quickly fell into a routine. The first task at hand was for me to file for disability. To do that, I had to acquire an ID and get a Social Security card. I had nothing. I started by contacting Wisconsin, and after jumping through some hoops, I was able to get a copy of my birth certificate sent to me. I eventually got all the required identification and made my way to the Social Security office. When it was my turn, the man asked me several standard questions. He finally asked what I had been doing for the last five years. I told him I had been homeless and living in the wilderness. He immediately looked up from his desk and said, "You better have a bank account set up because I am going to fast-track your application."

A few weeks later I got my check. It was a fairly large amount. They had gone back to the first time I applied all those years ago in the group home. I was able to pay all my back child support and had a fair amount left over. I got my own place right across the street from Jeannie. I could not have been more elated. I had been seeing a psychiatrist and was taking meds. I still hallucinated, and for some days the paranoia was crippling, but just knowing I had a safe place to stay was helping me a lot. Money was tight, but I was getting by. The first few months in my place were relatively uneventful.

I have always had a tendency toward manic behavior and it has gotten me into trouble periodically. At this time, I was taking my medication regularly, but as sometimes happens, my meds began to quit working as effectively. Before I knew it, I was frantically planning another backpacking trip, not for years this time, but for weeks. I was going to do the Ozark Highlands Trail, which was about 300 miles round trip through the mountains. In a way, I was still fresh out of the wilderness. Since I had been solivagant for so long, it just made sense to me. Jeannie drove me to the trailhead, and after making sure I had my meds with me, she said goodbye and gave me a big hug.

It was good to be back in the wild. I was diligent about taking my meds and was just enjoying the wilderness around me. It was especially nice to have an actual trail this time. It was late fall, so I was comfortable and well. I had periodic visits from Claire and Fred; murmurs a few times, but for days at a time, it was just me and the trees. I made it to the end and turned around to head home. After a few days, I thought it would be a good idea to restock some of my emergency supplies. Mostly, I was just craving coffee. There was only one store along the trail, in a little town called Oark, about 6 miles from the trail. I stepped out onto the highway, and before long, was sipping coffee at the general store.

A large man with a dark beard and clad in overalls walked up from down the dirt road that ran alongside the handful of homes in town. There wasn't much here. The general store and a few houses. There wasn't even a church, and for the Bible Belt, that was saying a lot.

"Hi, where are you headed?" He said in a deep voice.

"Just in from the Highlands trail, I was craving coffee..." I said with a smile.

"Haha, now that I understand! Name's Tim..."

I told him my name, and we began talking. I told him all about my travels out west, Laughing Cloud, Death Valley, and the horse ranch. He seemed especially keen on the horse ranch.

"So, you're a hard worker then?"

"I would say so, yes. I like to do a good job."

"I don't know what your plans are, but judging by that pack and your stories, you've been around for quite a while. If you'd like a place to settle for a few months, I could sure use your help." I don't know what came over me, but I asked with a smile, "What did you have in mind?" It must have been the mania or maybe I was just looking for a new adventure.

Tim elucidated that he had a house he was hoping to rent out. It was livable but needed a fair amount of work. He would let me stay there, plus give me a decent wage until the work was done. He assured me that I would be busy for at least two months. I finished my coffee and we walked down the dirt road together, arriving at a white house at the end of the road. It was barely visible behind all the overgrowth. We went inside. It wasn't terrible, but it sure did need some cleaning and paint. The first night in that run-down house, I sat out in the backyard, looking at the shadow of the mountains, wondering what would become of me.

I spent two months there getting to know Tim and his family well. His wife's parents were elderly and lived on top of the mountain north of town. One night, there was an ice storm. Tim woke me up before dawn, urging me to get ready quickly and to dress warmly. His wife's parents had lost power and were low on firewood that was near the house. We spent the entire day making our way up that mountain road, chopping up fallen trees with chainsaws, moving them aside, and going up to the next one. We finally made it to the top around dinner time. The power was still out, and they were burning the last few pieces of wood that were stored on the porch. They had more in the shed, but Pap had already fallen on the ice trying to get to it. After clearing the road, we had a truckload of wood we had gathered. Tim immediately put me to work splitting and stacking the logs on the covered porch. I felt like a hero that day. They were so grateful, and we really did save the day. Just as we were getting ready to head back down, the power came back on.

Feeling a sense of accomplishment after helping the elderly couple, Tim dropped me off at the house and drove back to his home. I was exhausted and feeling a little off. I didn't think too much of it because I was starving. I started some soup. I had been out of meds for a few weeks and the off feeling was getting more and more pronounced. Suddenly, just as my soup was done, Drake returned. I HATE YOU. YOU'LL NEVER BE GOOD FOR ANYONE. YOU SHOULD KILL YOURSELF. DO IT. END IT ALL NOW.

I huddled in the corner of the darkened kitchen of that white house at the end of the road. I had no radio or television to distract or soothe me. I was too afraid to leave and seek help. It was cold and icy outside, and it slowly turned into another one of the longest days of my life. I'm grateful that nobody came over, to find me shaking and crying like that, but I kind of wish someone had. I knew that being without meds was not a good path to be on.

Drake hammered away at me relentlessly for hours. Just when I didn't think I could take it anymore, he stopped. The insulting daggers shut abruptly off and caught me by surprise. The jolting quiet was almost equally alarming. The shouting had been going on for so long, that the sudden silence felt like stepping into a deep freeze on a hot day. I was completely on edge, not just from the verbal assault, but from the unexpected stillness. I was anxiously anticipating his voice to come roaring back to life at any moment. It never did.

A few days later, I was in the store having coffee when Paula came in. I knew her from passing, but not really what she did. I overheard her talking to the girl at the counter about the upcoming season at the adventure center. I was intrigued. I got up and went over to her.

"You've been helping Tim...."

"Yes, and I've been thinking about heading back, but not sure what is left for me there."

"Well, I can offer you free camping, food and showers, and a job until late fall."

Before I even knew what the job entailed, I agreed and was in her truck heading to the adventure center. It was only a couple of miles out of town, right along the bank of the beautiful Mulberry River. She showed me around, I set up camp at a private site a short distance away from the campground, and I got to work.

I spent spring, summer, and fall there working on canoes, running a zip line, and doing security for concerts. I thought about my kids a lot, and of Jeannie, who was probably wondering what had happened to me. The hallucinations were often a daily event, but most days I was on my own, working on whatever project I had been assigned for the day. I was also able to purchase an MP3 player and headphones. I used Paula's computer to download a bunch of songs. Having the soothing rhythms of music again was more amazing than I could have possibly imagined.

Since the early days of my childhood, music has always been a haven for me. Often, it had been my only refuge. The summer and fall went relatively well for me. It was late November, so I was finally getting ready to head out because the season was ending. I was organizing my things with plans to leave the next day when an older woman came up and started asking about trails in the area. I told her of a few and she admitted she wasn't a very accomplished hiker. She then asked if I would be willing to take her on a guided hike if she paid me. I pondered the idea for a moment, and then thought, sure, why not? We made our way up away from the river to the top of the ridge. I was leading but making sure to stay at her pace. We talked a lot. I mentioned I wasn't sure what was left for me in Fort Smith or where I would go next. She shared that she wanted to come back to this area because it was so beautiful. After a while, I could tell that she was beginning to tire, so I took a spur trail back to the main one, and we were heading back to camp when she asked,

"What if you had a place to stay for a while?"

"Well, that would be great, not sure where that would be, but I don't have a lot of prospects at the moment..."

"I have a cabin up near Devil's Den. It's remote but has water and power. There's even a creek on the property. It needs a little work, but you would be welcome to stay there until you got on your feet."

"Really, wow, that would be wonderful, I don't know what else to do, so I guess it's a yes from me."

"Great, the only thing is, I'm leaving today. I could drop you by there, but we must go soon."

I was used to spur-of-the-minute changes by this point, so I gathered my things, and before I knew it, we were off.

28

THE MANIC CABIN

Solitude vivifies; isolation kills.

Joseph Roux

The cabin was remote. It was located down the side of a mountain from the road that ran along the top of the ridge. There was power and water, even a TV and VCR with several movies, but not much else. We stopped along the way and she bought me a fair amount of groceries. I offered to pay for them, but she insisted. She even got me a small burner phone so I could call her if anything was amiss. I accepted this last gift with great trepidation. My paranoia was relentless about cell phones. I kept it in the package. After she left, I took it apart and never even turned it on. I ended up staying there much longer than I had expected.

I watched the winter come and go. Winters have always been tough for me. From an early age in Wisconsin, where it was too cold to stay out for very long, winter meant being stuck inside with a verbally abusive mother. I despised everything about it. It made me feel trapped and vulnerable. Surprisingly, it wasn't until I began the process of writing this book, at age 50, that I started to release a lot of those childhood demons. For the first time in 45 years, I was able to look forward to and embrace the glory of winter. My main purpose in writing this book is to help people, but in doing so, I have also helped myself. Although it has been a challenging process, it has been a very cathartic and empowering experience.

As spring turned to summer, I was getting antsy. I had been talking about getting a bicycle and checking out some of the mountain roads around the area. The kind woman would periodically visit to bring me food and books. On one visit she surprised me with a nice bike, helmet, and a few other goodies. I was overjoyed. I was off and pedaling as soon as she left. I began to bike more and more, eventually going as far as Eureka Springs. It was about 160 miles round trip through the mountains. One day, I headed out and biked the entire 160 miles in a single trip. Yep, I was manic again.

I biked to Fayetteville and bought some bags for the rack on the back of my bike. On a random day in June that year, when it was ungodly hot, I loaded up my bike and took off. I headed west. I had a small bike computer, and before I knew it, I had gone 100 miles for ten days straight. 1,000 miles of manic pedaling. I was somewhere in Kansas again, and quite literally out of my mind, but I kept going. Eventually, the mania subsided. I was deep in the southwest corner of Kansas and was having horrifying hallucinations that the FBI was following me around town. Their vehicles were everywhere. I saw agents in the bushes and behind trees. I kept dodging them, turning down different streets, but they were always around the next corner. I eventually ditched my bike, and still wearing my unstrapped helmet, ran into the ER shouting that I needed asylum.

It took several nurses, a shot of something, and over an hour to calm me down. Eventually, a psychiatrist came in, asking me questions like:

"Why do you think they were following you?"

"Can you tell me who the president is?"

"How did you get here?"

I was eventually admitted to the state mental hospital. The fear of getting locked up forever was bearing down on me like a runaway train. I couldn't think of anything else. It was completely unbearable. They had me doped up on some hefty meds, which made my hallucinations and paranoia better but kept me in a zombie-like haze most of the time. Despite the drug-induced state, the fears remained like bricks in a wall that went up around me. It shut everything else out but also trapped me in a dungeon of my own making.

The single salvation for my stay there was music. In a separate building, once a day, we would all be ushered off to make art. In a small room off to the side was an upright piano. I remarked on it and kept asking if I could play it. Eventually, while everyone else was drawing, I was playing. I had not played music in so long. It flowed out of me in great swells and fits. For an hour each day, nothing mattered except the song in my head.

While I was there, I was subjected to weekly rounds of electric shock therapy. It's not as bad as you see in the movies – it's worse. The continual shock and convulsions were bad enough, but afterward, I was a complete vegetable for a few hours. After that, my thoughts would flutter away like moths. You know that feeling when you walk into the kitchen for something, and your mind completely goes blank? I was in a constant state of that for days. Just when I started to feel more like myself, it was time for another treatment. I was there, under this regimen, for several months. Eventually, I was deemed well enough to be released and was headed on a bus back to Arkansas.

While I had been gone all that time, I was evicted from my place. Jeannie had managed to get in and save a few of my things, but for the most part, everything was gone. I stayed in her guest room for a few months, helping around the house, and mostly staying close to home.

Occasionally I drove Jeannie's car and gradually got bolder in venturing out. I mostly went to the store, but occasionally to a drive-through to grab a meal. As I was driving back to the house one day, I swerved to avoid a car that was crossing the center line. I barely nudged the car next to me. There wasn't much damage, but I quickly started to realize, the car that I had swerved to avoid wasn't even there. I was too afraid to say anything about it to anyone, so I passed it off to the other driver by saying I was distracted by a bee. A few weeks later, I was in the car again approaching an intersection. Suddenly a horse came galloping in from the left side. I swerved and hit the car next to me pretty hard. When the police came, I was out of the car running around trying to catch the horse. There was no horse. The officer must have had some mental health training because he assured me that they would take care of the animal and that I needed to go to the ambulance. He was very kind and treated me with dignity.

The ambulance took me directly to the fourth-floor mental health wing of the hospital. While I was there, I was visited by my psychiatrist. She informed me that she was putting in a recommendation to suspend my license. At first, I was really upset. I came around quickly when I realized that I could have badly hurt someone or worse. I'm grateful that I didn't. Soon after, a court date was set, and I lost my license.

29

IN THE MIDST OF THINGS

Life is what happens while you are busy making other plans.

John Lennon

Life settled down for a while and I eventually met a girl online and we started dating. Things were pretty good with her, but I realize now I was nowhere close to ready for a relationship. I kept her at a distance and hid large parts of myself from her. There were days I was suffering with symptoms but said nothing. I would isolate myself with music or pretend to be asleep. She knew I had schizophrenia but had no idea how bad it was. Eventually, we moved in together to a small mountain town that was pretty remote. It was about a 30-minute drive to my doctor, so it was a lot to ask her to do.

We were together for about a year. During this time, her 10-year-old daughter had a growing resentment of me. I did nothing wrong. If anything, I was overly kind and patient, but I just wasn't her dad. She wanted her parents back together and saw me as the reason they weren't. After a while, we realized her daughter was increasingly agitated about the situation and it wasn't healthy for any of us. We decided to go our separate ways. I wasn't terribly hurt; I knew that it was for the best. We parted cordially and I was on my own again. This time, I was sequestered in a secluded mountain town with no way of getting to my doctors' appointments. I asked my friend Denny a few times, but it always seemed like a big hassle for him. Eventually, I stopped going, which meant I stopped taking my meds. I had been down this road before many times in my life and it always led to disaster.

It needs to be said and I can't stress enough how important it is, but I want to take a moment to point it out here. STAY ON YOUR MEDS. The path without them is a dark one and can have grave consequences for you and the people you love. You should work with your doctor to strive for the best quality of life possible but do not stop taking your medications. Have a friend or loved one monitor you if you need to. If you live alone, have a routine, alarms, notes, whatever you need to do to stay on them. If your doctor is not listening to you, communicate or search for a better doctor, but don't stop your meds. I have learned that, just as a cancer patient does, I need to take mine to stay alive.

Money was extremely tight, and I was forced to trap rabbits and fish in the mountains to supplement my food supply. Being off my meds has always been difficult. With the isolation of being in the mountains, I felt like I was backpacking all over again. My symptoms were rampant and I struggled daily with anxiety and paranoia.

It was a hard winter and I huddled in the dark often with no food and abrasive voices. I thought at any moment they were going to break down the door and take me away. Spring finally came and I ventured out more and more online. I met another girl and we dated for a few months. She lived in a cool, artsy tourist town called Eureka Springs and eventually, I moved there. Eureka was wrought with late nights at bars around town. I stayed up for days at a time. My manic brain was filled with constant ideas about music and outlandish schemes. At one point, I was completely delusional and believed someone was contacting me from New York about a record deal. I read and responded to emails and completely believed it was real for several weeks. When I am unmedicated, I am extremely manic, outgoing, and always willing to take risks. The music scene there was thriving, so I buried myself in that world and tucked away the constant torture of my mental delusions and symptoms.

30

SEARCHING

*Beauty is beauty because beauty is temporary,
and beauty is temporary because we are temporary.
To seek beauty was to seek an affirmation of life,
even as you knew it wouldn't last.*

Brad Mehldau

I started playing bass in 2016. I purchased an unlined fretless ESP model. At the time, I was playing acoustic guitar around town and had always dabbled with the piano. From the moment I picked up the new bass and strummed the first note, it felt like home. There was instantly something that resonated with me in a way that is difficult to put into words. I had coined the phrase, "Music is the soul out loud." This was the first time I *felt* it. I immediately put away my guitar and piano and didn't touch anything but the bass for many years.

One of my favorite jazz musicians was a bass player. Jaco Pastorius is known by many as the best and most influential bass player ever. He was a bit of a personal hero to me. I have always loved his creativity and outstanding musicianship. He also suffered from mental illness. He led a tumultuous life and his illness eventually corrupted his mind. He exhibited erratic and destructive behavior at times and was finally diagnosed with bipolar. His struggle and rapid decline ended tragically and that has always served as a lesson to me to fight hard to manage my own schizophrenia. Jaco was known for being a pioneer of the fretless electric bass. So, when I began playing, I also wanted to play fretless. The character and sound of a fretless is not only unique but feels more.... personal. It is also more challenging, especially on an unlined fretless bass.

At this same time, I was still dating the girl I had met. We lived in a groovy attic apartment above a house filled with musicians. I picked up bass fast and spent an insane number of hours working on it. I was very superficial in my emotions with her. I skipped along the surface of our entire relationship, eventually slowing, and then quite suddenly, I sank. She endured my manic ways and eccentric behaviors. I was hypersexual and stayed up for days at a time recording music or going for long hikes in the dark. I was playing almost constantly, so I got pretty good on the bass in a short amount of time. Soon, I was playing around town with various individuals. She was not very supportive of this or of my music in general. Much like I had used running in my 20s, music quickly became an avoidance behavior.

Despite all of this, we got married. It was such a whirlwind relationship. I had no business tying the knot with the state I was in, but I desperately wanted to be loved. At the time, I didn't realize I was going about it completely the wrong way. I didn't understand that to be truly loved, I had to love myself. I was so far removed from that truth. Sadly, I despised myself. I hid in a fury of activity; not really knowing, much less loving, myself at all.

Eventually, her job wasn't working out and we moved to another town and lived upstairs in her parents' house. We were only there for a few months, but it was incredibly difficult. Her mom was skeptical and said quite often she didn't believe in mental illness. Her dad was a bit indifferent, but easygoing and much easier to be around. I spent most of my time either hiking around town or staying upstairs playing my bass.

One day, I was practicing in the bedroom with headphones on and had the door shut. Suddenly, I heard loud banging and saw the knob of the door twisting back and forth. I took off my headphones, and the banging persisted. I also heard loud voices on the other side of the door who were speaking in an aggressive tone. This went on for what seemed like forever. Things got worse when a hammer or something started smashing through the door. I hid down behind the bed not knowing what else to do. I was gritting my teeth and rocking back and forth. Suddenly, everything stopped. I listened closely, expecting footsteps to come across the floor to where I was hiding. There was nothing. Finally, after quite some time, I peeked over the bed to see the door perfectly intact. I had hallucinated it all. I will never forget that day. I was terrified and traumatized to be in that room for weeks afterward. Eventually, all that was going on got to be too much and I checked myself into the hospital again. I was there for several weeks but was disconcerted when my wife only visited me once. I was hurt, but it definitely let me know where we stood.

While I was in the hospital, the doctor prescribed a particularly assertive antipsychotic medication. It drastically reduced my hallucinations, but I became lifeless and sleepy all the time. It made me into a drooling zombie. I was a different person when I was released. I went from being manic, energized, hypersexual, and outgoing, to lethargic and quiet. Barely engaging with anyone, I would just sit and stare into space. I also gained a large amount of weight in a short amount of time. It was a dramatic turn and I can't blame her for reacting the way she did.

We quickly became more and more estranged, and eventually, she said she wanted a divorce. I put up no fight. On the day of court, she offered to drive me there. It was about a 20-minute drive from the apartment. Being in a courtroom with police and cameras all around, my anxiety was extremely high.

After court, she told me she was going to lunch and that I would have to find my own way home. I just walked away. I had $30, no phone, it would be dark soon, and I was 25 miles from my apartment. Panic set in. I had an aggressive panic attack behind a nearby restaurant. I slowly gathered myself and went to the library to see if I could find a phone. Nope. I had another panic attack in the bathroom. Finally, I made my way to the town square and got up the courage to ask a younger couple if they had a phone I could borrow to call a cab. Soon, I was on my way home. I walked in, locked the door, and cried.

I think a lot of people have misconceptions about people who are on disability. Maybe they think we are lazy or that it must be nice to just hang out all day. Without structure and with an overthinking mind, the days all run together. It is hard enough to feel like you don't have a purpose but add mental illness, anxiety, and agoraphobia to that mix, and it's a dangerous combination. The sheer isolation can be crippling.

The apartment was hell. The neighbors were extremely loud, fighting and banging on the walls at all hours. I continuously hallucinated people breaking in the front door, sometimes several times a week. I had daily symptoms of voices, paranoia, and anxiety. I could barely leave the apartment. I weighed myself one day and was mortified to see the small screen display the number 297. I called my doctor and told her it was time for a change.

The zombie med I was on caused me to swell up to the biggest I've ever been. I refused to get to 300 pounds. I started setting the timer on the oven, and walking laps around the apartment for 40 minutes, several times a day. I also did pushups and sit-ups. I started eating better. I fasted often and resumed meditation. The hallucinations and loud neighbors didn't go away, but at least I was getting healthier.

As I mentioned, one of the hardest things to deal with while being on disability is a lack of purpose. It's hard facing each new day feeling like you are contributing absolutely nothing. Fear kept me trapped in my apartment all day, wasting away mentally and physically. I had nothing driving me. No reason to exist.

I decided to start reaching out to people online. I began helping friends with issues they were having. For whatever reason, they all happened to be women. I think women tend to be more open about discussing problems or mental health issues. I had no romantic inclinations towards any of them. I was too focused on fixing their problems. I realize now it wasn't healthy for anyone, but it gave me a reason to get up every day. It was something that I could point to and say, 'Look, I helped over there...'

It took a big toll on me. I was absorbing their troubled energies and constantly thinking about solutions to their issues. A few had problems within their marriage; one was also a schizophrenic. I was running away all over again. I was investing completely in the world happening around me while ignoring the one I was living in. Helping them took me away from where I was, much like a gripping book does. Suddenly, I wasn't stuck. In my mind, I would visit, look around, and offer advice. I was certainly in no place to offer advice to anyone. I may not have helped at all. But for a time, it gave me a purpose, albeit one of deflection and distraction.

There were a few times I would venture for a walk outside, often at three or four in the morning to avoid contact with people. I had to go out once a month in the daytime to get my meds at Walmart. I despised that day but was committed to staying on my meds. One day I was on my way there, when suddenly small creatures made of fire emerged from the yard I was walking past. They started jumping at me, burning me anywhere they landed. It hurt and I was terrified. I rolled around in the yard swatting at them and yelling. At some point, the police showed up, and I was quickly placed in a rescue squad. I was taken to the hospital but was only there for a week. My amazing doctor showed up right away, adjusted my medication, and then signed my release.

I owe a tremendous thank you to Dr. Donna Rocha. She has hit one home run after another with my medications and treatment. Most of all, she is always a vigilant listener and goes above and beyond by asking my opinion of what would be best. She is the only doctor I have ever had that does this. I truly believe that I would not be living the best of my days without her help and guidance.

After my experience with the last two relationships, I vowed to myself I would never again be in that situation. My mantra every time I looked in the mirror was 'single forever.' I was content with this, working on myself, and not having to hide parts of myself or my symptoms from anyone.

In addition to my monthly excursion to Walmart, I also had to venture out for monthly appointments with my therapist and doctor. Medicare doesn't allow you to have both scheduled on the same day, so you must endure the extra burden of duplicative costs for a cab and suffer through two different trips that can be extremely stressful when you find it hard to leave the house.

On one of my trips to the doctor's office, I was sitting quietly in the waiting room. Suddenly, bullets started flying through the windows and hitting the wall. There was a shooter. I yelled for everyone to get down. I heard screaming. I piled furniture up in front of the windows. Eventually, I was wrestled to the floor by two men. I was sedated and placed in a locked room. There was no shooter. My meds were adjusted, but I didn't have to go to the hospital. After I calmed down, one of the nurses gave me a ride home.

Around this same time, I experienced another hazard of living alone coupled with the instability of schizophrenia. I must have hallucinated talking on the phone with Dr. Rocha about switching my medication. She said I was to take my new medicine once a day. I was currently taking my meds three times per day. I didn't realize I never actually had this conversation with her and consequently never switched my meds. I started taking only one pill instead of three because of my confusion. My symptoms escalated. During my next appointment, the issue was clarified and I went back on the proper dose. This was just one more example of how dangerous it can be for those who live alone or have no one to check in on them. Developing a consistent routine that ensures medication is being taken as prescribed is a critical part of the path to a better quality of life for anyone struggling with mental illness.

I have always been very diligent about my routine. For the most part, it has helped me stay on track with taking my meds and everything else related to my health. I have alarms set for each time of the day when I am supposed to take my meds. I also have a system that includes an elaborate pill case. I also set alarms for household chores and treat my daily life much like you would a job. This is important for people on disability, as the lack of structure can derail any notions of self-improvement or even something as simple as personal hygiene.

My relationship with two of my children deteriorated around this time. Things were not good when I returned from my backpacking trip. They were all young when I left and it was hard for them to understand why I had. When I got back, I reached out to them via handwritten letters and they responded. We then moved to calls and the occasional video chat. Still, to say that we were close after all that had happened would be a stretch. I don't fault them one bit, I completely understand their point of view. I can't imagine what it would have been like to have a parent disappear like that. Even as much as I despised my mother, it would have been hard not knowing where she was or if she was even alive or dead.

Around Christmas of 2019, my oldest daughter asked for a cease in communication, which I have honored. It's been hard, but I don't want to cause her any further distress. My son hasn't specifically asked for no contact but hasn't responded to my occasional messages since around that same time. I know that I can't push. All I can do is hope. Maybe one day they will read this book and glean a greater understanding of why I did what I did. I do know that I love them dearly and I always will.

I talk regularly to my daughter, MarKatie, our middle child, and that always brings me great joy. It's wonderful to see her blossom into being an amazing wife and mother of her own children. I'm grateful for every chance I get to speak to her. As of this writing, she has two daughters who are just as beautiful and vibrant as she is. Her husband is a great guy and it is awesome to see them all doing so well.

Out of all the things that schizophrenia has stolen from me, the theft of my children has been the most painful. It has been the biggest heartache of my entire life. My true hope in writing this book is that someone will read it, and when confronted with their own mental health difficulties, will make better decisions than I did. Through sharing what happened to me, I can take the fight against mental illness from my limited sphere and share it with the world.

31

BEGINNING TO BELIEVE

Everything you want is on the other side of fear.

Jack Canfield

At one of my therapy visits, my therapist suggested an exercise. She wanted me to reach out on Facebook to three people and tell them that I had schizophrenia. They had to be people that I didn't know very well. I had not been remotely public about my mental illness, and my paranoia was still high. The thought of putting myself out there like that made me very anxious.

Despite feeling very uncomfortable about reaching out to near strangers, I went home, summoned my courage, and picked three people off my contacts list. The first was a musician that I had met who struggled with depression. He had reached out to me before and I felt he would be receptive to me creating a dialogue. The second was a friend from Wisconsin whom I had known since college. He and I spoke periodically about our lives, but I had never spoken to him about my mental illness.

The third was Lesli. It took her a bit to respond to my message. We had initially connected on Facebook through a mutual friend, Vanessa. Vanessa and I had gone on one date many years prior. About halfway through the date, we were watching TV and suddenly, five or six small dragons were running and fluttering about in my kitchen. She was very concerned, so she stayed long enough to make sure I was okay. After such a jarring dating experience for both of us, we decided to stay friends but never went on another date.

In my initial message to Lesli, I mentioned it would be great to meet for coffee or tea the next time she was in town. She kindly agreed to let me know the next time she was going to be in the area. Our messages were all very positive and friendly. We started out talking about music, exercise, and weather preferences. Shortly after we started chatting, I told her about my schizophrenia. She was pretty sure that she already knew but wasn't sure how. I certainly wasn't public with it at that time. She was instantly compassionate and supportive, so I was relieved. The weight from the fear of opening up was lifted.

Not much more than a week or so into my conversations with Lesli, I began to share completely. Our talks were so effortless and organic, so it just flowed out of me naturally. I had never done that before, not even with doctors or therapists. It was the greatest feeling in the world to embrace the fear of being exposed, bear my darkest and scariest moments, and be supported and cared about at every turn. She never once doubted or dismissed me. She knew that I was struggling constantly. She saw the light in me from the very beginning, even when all I could see was darkness.

For several years before I met Lesli, I regularly hallucinated people breaking into my apartment. It happened over and over and completely fooled me every single time. They came when I was watching TV, cracking away at the frame of the door with a crowbar and twisting the door itself off the hinges. They came in the middle of the night when I was asleep. It was utterly terrifying every time. It is probably almost impossible to grasp what that was like. To me, it was totally real. I slept with the large hunting knife from my backpacking trip near my bed every single night. I did this even after I moved into Lesli's house. The amazing thing is, from the day I moved in with her, nobody ever broke in again. I was protected. I eventually put the knife in the closet.

I remember one night after I had been messaging Lesli for a few weeks. I was in my apartment watching television, when suddenly there was a commotion in my bathroom. I heard someone shuffling around in there and then the door closed. I was afraid and got up. I stood in the kitchen with a large knife, listening intently, and finally managed a "Hello?"

"I can't do this anymore. I have to end it all."

Her voice was weak and high-pitched. I could hear the agony in every syllable. There was more shuffling around and I heard something rubbing against the door. I gently said, "I don't know who you are, but it's going to be okay."

I was wondering if I should call the police at this point. Nothing in my life was normal, so when my mind is in this state, rational thinking doesn't connect correctly. I didn't stop to ask why or how this woman was in my bathroom, I just accepted that she was. In hindsight, it always sounds so weird, but in those moments, it just makes sense. I don't know how else to elucidate it. As I have mentioned before, it's kind of like when you are dreaming. No matter how bizarre your dream is, when you are in it, it seems perfectly normal and logical. It is only later, when you wake up, that you say, "What the hell was that?"

I messaged Lesli, asking her what I should do about this woman in my apartment.

```
Who is she? How did she get in?

I don't know, I don't know. I must have fallen asleep.
```

I tried to get her to tell me her name through the door. It was silent.

```
She won't answer. What if she's dead?

You are okay, she isn't there. You need to open the door and find that she isn't there.
```

Okay, I can do this. I took a few deep breaths and tried the door. It was locked. I had one of the little keys in my bedroom. I went to get it. When I returned, she was standing in the living room, blood dripping from her wrists and onto the floor.

"Oh my God, oh my God, let me help you!"

She said nothing, just looked down at herself and the blood pooling on the floor. I turned back to the kitchen to get some towels for her wrists. When I turned back around, she was gone. The blood was gone. There was no sign of her being there whatsoever. It was in that instant, I awoke from that nightmare of a dream. Except I wasn't dreaming. I was wide awake and hallucinating. I collapsed on the floor, I felt broken and crushed under the weight of my own mind. Part of me expected her to come back.

```
She's gone, she just disappeared.

I'm here for you, I can't imagine how terrifying that must have been. What can I do to help?

Just talk to me, about anything...
```

We messaged back and forth about music, which is always one of my favorite subjects. It truly has always been a refuge for me since I was a small child. As we continued to talk, I slowly started to relax, and the anxiety started to fade. In those moments, I knew that in her, I had found a living refuge. Min ekta hjem. For the first time ever, I no longer felt like a burden. I had a friend who was truly present and genuinely accepted me.

32

I AM...

*There are two ways of spreading light:
to be the candle or the mirror that reflects it.*

Edith Wharton

Lesli and I had talked for countless hours through Messenger but had never spoken over the phone. I still remember the surge of butterflies that rose up when we picked a day to call. It was a Wednesday. She said she would call when she was done with work and dinner.

My phone rang.

Unlike any other meeting in my life, this was a *reunion*. She had a light in her voice that was a complete joy to witness. For a few hours, my chaotic life disappeared, time stood still, and the ebb and flow of our voices reached in and lit up rooms in my heart that had been dark for my entire life.

She spoke with compassion and a willingness to understand that I had never before experienced with another person. My fear all but abandoned me in those moments. Not once did I worry or even wonder what she was thinking about me. From our first hello, I had complete trust and reverence for her.

I will never forget standing in my apartment kitchen around 11 p.m. that night. Our phone batteries were running low, and we were about to say our goodbyes when suddenly she said emphatically and full of inspiration,

"I want you to say, 'I am amazing!'"

Nobody had ever asked me to do such a thing before.

"C'mon Todd, let's hear it..."

"I am amazing."

"No, really say it! From your core, your soul, really mean it!"

"I am amazing!"

"Louder!"

"I AM AMAZING!!!"

"YES! That's it, come on, say it again!!"

In those moments, I began to believe in myself. It was only a small sliver of light coming in through the tiny cracks of the walls I had built around myself, but it was light. For the first time in my life, I reveled in the light of another person. I let her in. My fear of rejection and judgment vanished a little more each time I repeated it.

"I AM AMAZING!!"

"YEAH!!!"

The joy that surged through every pore of my body was electric. I felt an incredible release knowing that someone was able to see through my walls. I was slowly realizing that it was me, being truly seen for the first time.

The seed was planted. We talked about our lives, our families, our victories, and our failures. We talked until the battery of my cordless phone died. We couldn't stop sharing our stories. I got the other handset from the bedroom and called her back until that one died. We finally had to say good night and I remember lying in the bed feeling like my whole being had been awakened from a long dark slumber. It was as if someone had instantly flipped a light switch inside my soul.

The next day, I was off to get new phones. I barely left my apartment at this point, except to get meds, but I was determined to be able to talk to her. This meant a trip to Walmart, past the yard where the fire creatures had attacked me, past the busy road with all the cars and people, and into the den of a thousand cameras that we know as Walmart.

Before I ventured out, I had done my research and picked out the phones I wanted online. Since I didn't have a car, I made sure they were in stock since I couldn't just pick them up. I had to go into the store. With Brad blasting away in my headphones, I went in and made my way to the back of the store. The phones I had chosen were nowhere to be found. I quickly looked over the ones available because I was way too anxious to ask anyone for help. I made my selection and nervously waited at the checkout. As I stood there, I was frantically considering every single camera that was trained on me. I kept wondering who was watching, fighting the paranoia that was slithering up the back of my neck like a cold malleable hand. Finally, I was out. The breath of fresh air felt like life itself reentering my body.

I wasn't running then, but I certainly felt like it at that moment. It was times like this that my anxiety would temporarily slip away. My feet didn't feel the ground as I reveled in my victory, carrying my new phone like a world record trophy.

It's always been important for me to celebrate every victory, no matter how small. I've always just wanted to be able to do what 'normal' people do. The thought of being able to go into a store without the stressful weight of fear and anxiety was impalpable at that time. That would come later. However, I did know how important it was to acknowledge every step towards those goals. Journaling has been one way for me to document the journey. I keep track of all my successes, attempts, even failures, and second attempts. I have a running journal, a symptom journal, and one in which I just let my consciousness wander wherever it feels like going. For a long time, it was relatively impossible for me to journal my symptoms. My paranoia was too persuasive and I was afraid someone would read my journal. For a while after we met, Lesli kept track of my symptoms for me. She logged my hallucinations, panic attacks, and days I was plagued with voices. Having a detailed record of my symptoms allowed me to share them when I talked to my doctor. With the journal, I knew exactly what had happened and when. It became an invaluable tool and improved my treatment tremendously.

When I returned home from my victorious trip to Walmart, I sent Lesli a picture of me in the kitchen holding the new phones. She was so proud of me. She knew what a huge deal it was for me to take a spontaneous trip to the store. She has inspired and motivated me from the very beginning and continues to do so repeatedly. I learned the importance of *attempt small - celebrate big*. Feeling triumphant from the day, I talked to her for hours that night and cherished every single word.

I was getting bolder given the encouragement and support of my new friend. As my confidence slowly began to build, I went for walks more often, some even in the daylight. One day, I was coming around the corner in a subdivision, and police cars were lined up in the street. I stopped in sheer panic. I turned to go back the way I came, but more cars had come in behind me and were lined up there too. I was trapped. The police lights were flashing all around me. A few of the officers were standing near the vehicles and were pointing at me. I crumpled like a wet blanket and hid down behind a brick mailbox. I was shaking and knew at any moment they would come and get me and haul me away.

"Are you ok?"

My brain barely acknowledged the voice I heard, like a car door far off in the night. Still shaking, I eventually opened my eyes, to see an older man standing over me. He was keeping his distance but had a grave look of concern on his face.

"Yeah, um, I think so," I lied.

The police were gone. The quiet suburban neighborhood had returned. I got up, apologized, and took off at a brisk pace towards my apartment. I was sure they were going to reappear at any moment or be waiting for me when I got home. When the door shut and locked behind me, I was still trembling and watching intently out the windows. I called Lesli. Her voice washed over me like the sound of a gentle brook. She was reassuring, calm, and thoughtful - more than anyone had ever been.

I felt like I had been holding my breath for my entire life, and now, I could finally breathe. We shared so much in such a short amount of time, and it never felt like something new. It felt like a homecoming. I was diligent in my decision to stay single, however, so we kept everything strictly platonic. We both were finally starting to know what it was like to be 'seen' for the first time and cherished every moment we had exploring this new kindred friendship.

Eventually, we decided to meet in person and she came for a visit. I remember being incredibly nervous and telling her I was not sure if I would be able to meet her outside or not. I talked to her while she made the drive. When she arrived, I remember getting off the phone, taking a deep breath, and going down to the parking lot to greet her.

I was standing there when she pulled up and got out. In that instant, a part of me knew we would not be 'just friends' for very long. She was absolutely stunning with a radiant smile and eyes full of positive intention. She was the most beautiful poem I had ever seen. I wanted to be respectful though and honor our friendship. We hugged and I felt the greatest sense of joy I had ever experienced. We sat like old friends, played music, and shared about our lives. Around lunch, I wanted to go to a restaurant. Because of my anxiety and paranoia, this had been impossible to do for quite some time. I knew I could do it if she was there with me. We hopped in the car and headed to the local Subway. I was doing okay until a bunch of people came in behind us. She could tell I was struggling, so she gently put her hand on my shoulder and talked me through it. I was so close to bailing. Everything in me was screaming to run out of there, but I remained. With her beside me, I summoned my courage and took deep breaths like she advised and we were able to complete our order and leave calmly.

She was surprised when I decided I wanted to sit outside as opposed to going home. I shared with her then that all I ever wanted to do was what normal people do. Normal is such a relative term, but it gets the point across. Since the onset of my illness, I have yearned to be able to do what everyone else doesn't think twice about and takes for granted - things like leaving your apartment or ordering a sandwich. Being able to do anything without the constant battle of wondering if what you're witnessing is happening. On this day and every day since, Lesli has always celebrated every single victory with me. No matter how small, she has been there cheering me on. Perhaps more importantly, if I failed, she celebrated that I had even tried.

That night, we enjoyed cooking together, had a nice dinner, and spent the evening listening to music and talking. I had bought nice new pillows and sheets for her, so she could sleep in the spare bedroom. She stayed the night since we were planning to hang out the next day. She told me several months later when we closed our doors that night, she had the strangest feeling. She didn't want it to end. She wanted to open the door and come into my room and just lay next to me. She didn't know it at the time, but I wanted that too.

A few weeks before we met, I was feeling especially bold and had ventured out for a longer hike than usual. As I walked under a large tree, I heard a loud groaning and looked up. The branches were twisting. They were reaching down to me. Before I knew what was happening, they were all around me, trapping me under what was like a giant evil umbrella. I yelled. I tried to push my way through. It felt like I was stuck in there forever. By this time, I was on the ground, twisted and bent like car crash metal. Suddenly there was a loud whoosh and the branches all went back to where they had been. A runner had stopped and was looking at me with a concerned and somewhat scared look on her face. She came up to me cautiously and asked if I needed help.

"I don't know, I...."

Honestly, I don't remember much of what I said. The walk home was a whirlwind of fear and intrusive thoughts. After that terrifying experience, I didn't think I was going to be alive for much longer. I remember playing my bass for a long time when I got home.

During the second day of Lesli's visit, she and I walked to that same tree. I felt compelled to share with her where the agonizing event had taken place. We took our first picture together in front of the tree and reveled in my victory in overcoming past traumas. I was learning. Not just that it's important to keep striving to be the best version of yourself; I was learning what it meant to truly be me. The parts of me that I had hidden from the world for so long were being seen in the light by this beautiful person and celebrated for their truth, their strength, and quite simply because they were mine.

It was during this visit that I played my bass for Lesli. She was immediately taken by my playing, and we both enjoyed the experience. This sentiment would be echoed in the years to come every single time I played for her, which was often. I hadn't played for anyone but myself for quite some time. I was nervous, but her delight and compliments left me feeling encouraged and inspired.

For the first time in my life, I felt that I could completely open up to someone about everything. My day-to-day struggles with schizophrenia were a constant battle, but I shared them with her. She engaged completely and was encouraging and supportive in perfect ways. I shared more. It was as if the iron heel of oppression was suddenly lifted and I could see the sky for the first time. Deep within, I had finally found what makes me come alive.

33

LOVE

I love you completely and forever all at once.

Lesli Crush

The second time Lesli visited, we spent the day talking and listening to music. We took a nice long walk and made plans to cook that evening. All day long, we kept making excuses to get closer to one another, not realizing we were both feeling the same way. Even as friends, there was an undeniable connection. We took pictures and I moved the chairs in the living room right next to each other. We had a nice dinner together, cooking and moving about in the kitchen in sync. We settled in to watch the Jaco Pastorius documentary. A little way in, I laid my head on her shoulder. Unbeknownst to me at the time, she would reveal to me later that at the time I put my head on her shoulder, she had been thinking moments before about doing the same thing. Synchronicities like that happened frequently between us.

A bit later, she asked if it would be okay if we held hands. Ribbons of joy ran through me as I held her hand in mine. As the movie rolled past, the rest of the world disappeared, it was just her and me. For the first time in my life, I felt truly safe. Towards the end of the film, she looked at me and said "I kind of want to kiss you..."

With a determined posture, I stood up, took my glasses off, and kissed her. I couldn't stop. Time, as it does often with us, paused and waited for us to finish. I had never experienced a profound connection like that before. We kissed hundreds of times that night and went to bed with our clothes on, just holding each other and kissing like two high school kids making out for the first time. I hadn't slept through the night in probably ten years, but I did that night. I had been tormented by horrible dreams about my mother, voices, hallucinations of people breaking in, and the general loud chaotic environment of my apartment. But that night, I slept all the way through.

I was truly at home for the first time.

That first morning, waking up together, was nothing short of pure magic. My heart was at rest in the home of her soul. As I opened my eyes, joy enveloped me like the summer sun. I knew it was the first morning of the rest of my life.

The hardest part was watching her drive away. I knew that my life would never be the same, but I felt a closeness to her that I had never felt with anyone before. She had to go home to her daughter and her job, but all I could think about was seeing her again.

The dawn dissolved into the afternoon, and I was sitting in my usual spot in my chaotic apartment. I started to notice black SUVs in the parking lot. I didn't get up from my chair at first but got increasingly alarmed when agents in FBI jackets started milling about. Eventually, I could see they carried automatic weapons and wore bulletproof vests. I was positive they were coming for me. Again, my rational brain disengaged. I was back in the waking nightmare, where everything seemed normal, no matter how bizarre. They were all coming for me. I was sure of it.

I messaged Lesli. She was worried and asked me to take a picture. I snapped a shot through the tiniest slit in the blinds, and she responded.

```
I don't see anyone...

But I can see them in the picture!
```

My brain was surging with growing panic. She calmly talked to me. She urged me not to answer the door or look out the windows anymore. She guided me through the storm, reassuring me the FBI agents weren't there until my rational brain returned and I knew what was happening.

I played bass with my back to the wall so I could see all the entrance points. We messaged back and forth for a while. She stayed with me until I calmed down and started to feel better. Eventually, I looked outside again, and it was a normal parking lot. Nothing but ordinary cars. No black SUVs, no FBI. No one is coming for me. This was another huge victory and a big stepping stone for me. My trust in her allowed me to step away from the source of my panic and take a different path.

The next time she came to visit she brought her daughter, Jazmin, with her. I was nervous, as anyone would be, but for me, there was an added element. At 12 years old, she was about the same age as Claire. Kids have always made me anxious. I didn't know if she would like me or what she would be like. It had been quite some time since I had interacted with a young person.

When they arrived, I went to Jazmin's side of the car, said her name with a smile, and gave her a high five. I had debated this in my mind. A high five seemed fun and not as intrusive as a hug. It went well. We went inside and I was immediately set at ease by Jazmin. She was calm, considerate, and curious. We went for a walk together, down to the tree that attacked me. I thought about it but was confident that it wouldn't happen with them there. We took funny pictures and I quickly forgot all about the attack.

Lesli and I had already talked about me moving to her house. On the second day of their visit, I went into the spare bedroom and sat down with Jazmin. I told her of our thoughts about the move and that it would only happen if she was completely on board.

She agreed with no reservation and I was elated. It lifted my heart. Not just because of the feelings I had for Lesli, but because of the chance to share in parenting again. Schizophrenia had robbed me of being a father to my own children, stealing me away to the wilderness. This was a second chance at that indelible role. In every way, I knew that this was the right path for me, and us.

I remember an evening shortly after their visit. I was sitting in a chair, watching television, when something loud hit one of my windows. I thought it might be a bird since I was on the second floor, but the sound was more metallic than that. Before I could get up, a second *clack* and then a third. The blinds were closed, so I had no idea what was happening. Was someone throwing rocks at the windows? As unruly as the children were in this complex, it was not a big stretch.

I got up the courage to peek through the blinds. I made sure to shut off all the lights beforehand and crept to the window. With a trembling finger, I lifted the blind just enough to see the menacing eye of a drone glaring at me from just a few feet away. It immediately flew forward, crashing into the window right before my eyes. I screamed and fell backward onto the floor. I retreated to the bathroom since there were no windows and huddled in the dark. I could hear more and more of them crashing into the windows, trying to get in. I felt like any second one was going to crash into the bathroom door.

All of a sudden, there was silence.

I waited for what seemed like hours before venturing out far enough to see the front windows. I couldn't see anything, but I could hear the whirring of their propellers as they hovered. What were they waiting for? The phone rang. I darted to the kitchen half scrunched over. It was Lesli. I answered in a hoarse whisper.

"What's wrong?"

"Drones, there are drones everywhere trying to get in!"

"You're safe Todd, it's going to be okay. Don't look out the windows."

"Okay...okay..."

"Let's take some really deep breaths together."

"I don't; I..."

"C'mon, you can. There, good... Now, tell me about Jaco..."

She knew exactly how to soothe and distract me. She was never doubtful and delightfully patient. Before I knew it the whirring had stopped and I peeked out - no drones.

From the very beginning, Lesli was the perfect partner. She knew how to acknowledge my hallucinations without confirming or denying them. Her acceptance of how I was feeling was absolute and with the utmost compassion. Most of all, she knew how to distract me from what was happening perfectly. You don't have to be in a romantic relationship for this to happen. It could be a sibling or a friend. It only takes someone who knows that they don't have to cure you, they just need to be with you - someone who can take your thoughts away from the immediate nature of peril that you are witnessing and back to something that distracts you.

This method of distraction was very much in harmony with the coping skills I had developed before I met her, such as playing bass, doing math, running or hiking, and even something as simple as watching baseball and charting the balls, strikes, and outs. There was more brevity with her help though. I was able to get to that place of diversion faster. On my own, it took a while longer and I was quite worked up before I realized I needed to instigate a change. In both scenarios, distraction was a key element in my day-to-day life and continues to be to this day.

Our first kiss was on March 14th, 2020. I moved just two short weeks later on April 1st. For someone who had barely left their apartment for several years, packing up all my belongings and going to a place I had never been to would have ordinarily been quite a stressful event. I was a little nervous, but primarily filled with excitement and anticipation. My connection to Lesli was so strong and complete, I knew that no matter what happened, she would be with me every step of the way.

34

PANDEMIC

Life isn't about waiting for the storm to pass.
It's about learning how to dance in the rain.

Viviane Greene

I moved just as the onset of COVID-19 was gripping the world with fear and anxiety. In a lot of ways, the pandemic helped me with the transition. First, I didn't have to change doctors even though I was moving over an hour away. Telehealth had been approved so I could do my appointments from the couch. Second, it helped with Jazmin. She was home from school the first semester that fall, so we had the opportunity to grow close quickly. We worked on homework and ate meals together. The pandemic also limited the number of sleepovers she had. No one was spending the night with friends at the time. I was still not good with other people being in the house, so the minimized visits helped tremendously. My location may have changed, but my triggers to noise and strangers were still very visceral.

My first few weeks at the house were an adjustment, but a good one. I sure didn't miss the chaos of the apartment. It was especially nice to have a whole room just for music. In the apartment, I had to play in headphones all the time, which was difficult because I was always thinking that someone was going to sneak up on me. Now, I could play out loud throughout the day. Music became a coping mechanism in a whole new way all over again. I would learn songs during the day and then play them for Lesli when she got home from work.

I struggled a lot with leaving the house. I tried to go for daily walks, but it was not without struggles. I remember one incident where I was out walking and a man driving a white truck sat idling at an intersection while I approached, crossed, and continued. He then pulled onto the street and idled behind me. I quickly took a turn and started making a new route home. When I got there, he was in his truck parked on the street that ran along the side of our house. I locked the door and checked all windows. I called Lesli. She talked to me a long time about how it was probably just coincidence, and that he was probably a worker or something. She also raised the idea that it could all be a hallucination. This had not occurred to me. It rarely does. Again, my rational brain shuts off and I'm trapped in the reality of whatever my mind has constructed...just like a dream. I saw him several more times that first summer and it freaked me out every time. Eventually, I stopped seeing him.

This newfound role as a parent was not without great difficulty. I certainly was not used to the activities of a young adolescent. Because of my childhood, I had a distorted viewpoint about children. I was raised around the mindset that kids were to be controlled and kept in a place that denied them the ability to act out or be themselves.

For the most part, things were good for us, but just under the surface of myself, parts of me were boiling. I certainly wasn't verbally abusing Jazmin or locking her in a closet, but I found myself enraged whenever she would speak up for herself or get loud in her room. I didn't understand for the longest time why I was getting so upset. I was upset at my mother all over again and projecting it onto Jazmin because she was doing what I was never allowed to do. She was free to have the childhood I never got to have. This would be an ongoing issue and one that has finally evolved to a healthy understanding within myself as I sit here writing almost four years since that first meeting. I learned a lot from the experience of my backpacking trip. Through that ordeal, I learned above all, acceptance. I know that deep within me resides a peace that can only be tapped through that vein. I still get caught up in the moment from time to time but my understanding of situations that used to seem impossible has grown exponentially. Backpacking was the first piece of knowing myself. Meeting Lesli and Jazmin was the second. The final piece was writing this book.

The years with Lesli have been the most rewarding of my life. It has been an incredible journey, at times difficult, but in the end a very empowering and self-searching/healing sojourn. At the forefront of this journey was Lesli. Her strength, constant encouragement, and love have been the mainstays that have kept me going. At times, the things she said were difficult to hear, but I know that they were spoken with nothing but loving intentions and the desire to see me grow. The growth that I have experienced in a few short years is nothing short of a miracle. Jazmin has also been incredibly supportive, compassionate, and understanding. Without her openness and acceptance, our life together would never have transpired so quickly.

When I met Lesli, I was a shell surrounded by things constantly trying to break me. She was the one to come along and begin the process of breaking me wide open. She showed me that I was beautiful in all my brokenness. I did not like this process. It was uncomfortable, scary, and even embarrassing at times; but I embraced it. Not because it was all those messy things, but because, for the first time in my life, I was all of me. In that, I was truly alive for the first time.

The things that scare us, and I mean really scare us, are the closest to our truth. I'm talking about facing the worst parts of yourself, witnessing them, sharing them, and having the other person embrace all those parts of you that nobody (not even myself) had ever seen; until we can embrace and love those things about ourselves. In that moment, and only in that moment, will we be whole. The next part of this book will chronicle that journey. It will never be over, but in the last few years, I've traveled lifetimes within myself.

35

TRANSFORMATION

Life is one big transition.

Willie Stargell

In the spring of 2020, I moved in with Lesli and Jazmin. There was a tremendous amount of trust that was freely given between the three of us. It was truly remarkable and gave me a deep sense of comfort. For me, who barely ventured out of my apartment except to get my meds once a month, it meant putting my fears aside and putting love first, not just for them, but for myself. I knew that I couldn't stay where I was, and the compassion and love they both had shown me made me feel I could do anything with their support.

For Lesli and her daughter, it meant accepting all the ins and outs that came along with schizophrenia. It took me a while, but eventually, it hit home that it didn't matter. That I wasn't my illness, not to them. To them, I was kind, thoughtful, loving, and beautiful. I saw this in their eyes every single day, and after some time, I saw it in my own eyes when I looked in the mirror. Nobody had ever loved me in that way before. To be fair, I hadn't opened up to anyone either. It became clear that allowing myself to be seen completely was necessary for absolute love. It was their unwavering love that blossomed within me, providing the foundation for my transformation.

As I packed up my old apartment, surrounded by the chaos and endless noise of my neighbors, I felt anxious about the move but mostly had a growing enthusiasm about the change. I knew from the first time I talked to Lesli that my life would never be the same, even if she had remained nothing more than a great friend. Now, I knew that I had someone who would be there for me. She had shown me that at every turn.

Eventually, the day came, and we loaded up everything we could, and I left the rest. On the car ride south, I marveled at the quiet now that I was gone from that place. No more basketball in the hallway or violent arguments at all hours from the neighboring couple. Most of all, for the first time, I had a love that I could open to completely; and, in Jazmin, a second chance at parenthood.

It was everything I had imagined it to be and more. The quiet at night while I slept, with nobody banging on the other side of the walls. I felt safe. For the first time in decades, I lived in a space that physically, mentally, and in my heart felt like home. I was still not without difficulties. Much like I had learned on my backpacking trip, just because my body moves, does not mean that my hijacked mind gets left behind. All the anxiety and symptoms come with me, wherever I go.

In the beginning, I struggled to go to restaurants and stores because of my social anxiety. It's hard to put into words, but it was almost like there was a force vibrating the air in the room, like a loud vacuum cleaner grinding up bits of bone. The people, the noise, and the sensory overload were just too much to take most of the time. Jazmin did have friends over periodically and this was especially difficult for me. Her bedroom was directly above ours and I struggled with the noise. It seemed unfair to ask her and her friends to be quiet, but it was a trigger that I couldn't seem to shake for a long time. Jazmin was always very understanding and compassionate, so it made the transition so much easier.

During this time, I was taking medication for anxiety. Before I knew it, it had gotten out of hand. I would take it, forget I had taken it, get anxious again, and then double up. I had a 30-day supply and was running out in a little over two weeks. This went on for quite some time. It did help with the anxiety, but often it didn't make a dent, so I would retreat with my headphones and isolate myself. Eventually, Lesli helped me come up with a plan. I would have one pill available to me and she would have the rest with her in her purse. If I took it, it would be replaced the next day. This provided a valuable check for me and kept me from overusing the medication. I began to rely more on Lesli, breathing, and music for anxiety relief. They all helped. Breathing was certainly always available to me if I could remember to utilize it.

As I mentioned, I started playing bass in 2016. I had been playing piano and guitar up until that time, but nothing resounded the way bass did. I ordered a fretless bass to use on my recordings, but when I hit that first note, I put all the other instruments away. The bigger strings, the robust tones, the feel of the bare wood free of frets...it all just fit. I was relentless. I played at all times of the day. I would play for at least three and as many as eight hours every day. I seemed to be able to navigate virtually any style or difficulty of music on the bass much easier than any other instrument. I played for joy, for anxiety relief, for expression, for the challenge, and every time I played a note, my spirit was soothed.

When I was in my apartment, I couldn't play out loud because of my neighbors. I had negotiated with them to play out loud for one hour each day. The rest of the time was spent with headphones on, standing with my back in the corner so that I could see the door and windows. I was terribly afraid of someone sneaking up on me. Moving to Lesli's house created an amazing opportunity to play out loud every single day. I had a whole room dedicated to music. I was completely grateful to be able to play there, but I also loved that almost every night, I would play for Lesli and sometimes Jazmin. Nobody had ever taken that keen of an interest in my music before. It was supported and cherished.

Much as it had been when I was an abused child, music became an oasis all over again. From those early days when I was four at the piano until now, music gave and gave. I can't recall a single incident where it took away. When I started playing bass, I got deeper and deeper into jazz. This led me to the great jazz pianist, Brad Mehldau. He plays with a rhythmic and harmonic complexity that is unmatched by anyone I've ever heard. At first, even ballads of his were difficult. I persevered. Even now that I can play along relatively well with most of his catalog, I hear new things every single time. I recently read his book and learned of his struggles with childhood abuse and addiction. Along with Jaco Pastorius, he is my other musical mentor.

Brad has saved my life more than once. There have been several times when my symptoms were so severe, I felt I had no escape. Somehow, I managed to drag myself through the teeth of the storm in my mind and find my way to my bass. I created a playlist on my iPod years ago called, "Clear the Mechanism." It's where I go when my mind is hijacked, when I feel hopeless, or during the times when I am close to ending it all. Brad is featured prominently on that playlist. I remember those moments at the brink like I do any one of my near-death experiences. I'm thankful to have survived those dark interludes and grateful to him for providing the soundtrack for me to heal. There have been several times I was suicidal, and with Brad's help, I pulled myself...note by note...back from the edge. Back to a place where I may not know what will happen to me next, but where I have hope again.

Music engages a part of my mind that I can't reach any other way. At times, I can't feel my feet on the floor or the rest of my body; I only feel my hands and the vibrations of my fretless bass. It knows the theme of my soul. I would highly encourage anyone to learn to play an instrument. You don't have to be a master musician to seek solace in the fulfillment that comes from it. The satisfaction and joy that come from making an inanimate object sing with the melody of your song is resounding and powerful. Even if you never play for anyone, learn to play for you.

 I play differently when I am in psychosis. I was unaware of this for a long time since I was almost always struggling with symptoms and didn't have the means to record myself. Once I was able to make a recording, I discovered I take more risks musically when in psychosis. Almost as if my mind makes connections that I wouldn't normally explore. My sound is edgier and more angular, and my voice on the instrument is more broken up, almost like there's more than one of me playing.

 As we settled into our new routine, our partnership continued to deepen in understanding and personal growth. On May 14th, 2020, I had a plan. After dinner, I invited Lesli up to the music room so that I could play for her. I was nervous, but also so completely excited I could barely stand it. As the first song played, I was intentionally not playing well. I played the wrong notes and my timing was poor. I switched to the next song, saying, "I just can't seem to get that one right, I don't know what's happening…"

 She smiled and seemed a little concerned. If I was one thing, I was always practiced. I prepared relentlessly every day, and wrong notes were certainly a rarity. Bad timing never happened.

 I started in with the next song and continued intentionally playing badly. I stopped after a few moments and set down my bass. I walked over to the chair where she was sitting and got down on my knee. With trembling hands, I pulled the small box out of my pocket. I said, "I just can't play these songs any longer until I know that you are going to be my wife."

 I will never forget the look of complete love and acceptance that came across her face. We kissed like we never had before. I had been waiting for her my entire life. I knew she had been waiting for me too.

 I had another surprise in store and this one was for Jazmin. We went downstairs where she was sitting at the kitchen table. I went up to her and got down on my knee. I said, "Jazmin, I asked your mom to marry me and she said yes! You are an indelible part of this too, and I wanted to ask if you would welcome me into your life as well."

 With that, I produced another small box containing a pair of diamond earrings. She said, "Yes, yes of course!" and gave me a big hug. I could see the genuine joy in her expression and feel the weight of the moment for both of us.

I remember that day very well. There are things about it, like the way the afternoon sun was coming in the windows. I will always see that as a metaphor for letting people in. Since the day I met both of them, I have been growing - sometimes with difficulty, but growing, nonetheless.

Soon after we got engaged, I wrote down a plan for Jazmin to have friends over. It was a natural progression from one friend with Lesli there, to a few when I was there by myself. There wasn't a timeline, just a series of stepping stones. I went back and forth from one to another. I would try to forge ahead, but then couldn't do it and would back off to the previous step. It was very difficult for a long time. I'm sure that it was more than frustrating for Jazmin, but she never complained - not once. Her grace with everything that happened when I came into their lives is something for which I will forever be grateful.

Every time someone was coming over for the weekend, I agonized about it. The noise was troublesome and I knew that a part of me was upset because she was doing what I couldn't do as a child. I also had a general anxiety about having someone else in the house. I still do to this day. It has drastically improved, but I still have a base layer of uneasiness about visits. Jazmin was never resentful and never really pushed to go to the next step. Her compassion and understanding were truly remarkable. At every turn, she demonstrated a level of maturity that was far beyond her years.

We slowly started to venture out in public more frequently. Stores and restaurants were still a major challenge at this point. I struggled with the thoughts of strangers thinking about me, planning to hurt me and follow me home. It didn't help that there were cameras everywhere. I couldn't last in a store for more than a few seconds before the paranoid delusions of who might be behind the cameras took over. I think a big part of my angst was because, as a child, I perpetually felt like I had done something wrong. I was freakishly aware of every glance and focusing lens. I was convinced the police were going to come and haul me away at any moment.

Despite all the anxiety I experienced in public places and with guests in our home, when I eventually played music in public, all my anxiety disappeared as soon as I played the first note – proving the power of music. We had a running joke in the family that said, 'If Todd could just play bass while we ate at the restaurant, everything would be alright.' As time has passed, playing in public has become easier, but I'm still anxious until I hit that first note.

Music helped get me through the holidays that first year, too. We had a wonderful Christmas celebration at Lesli's mom's house, but I struggled with a house full of people. They were gracious enough to let me use a spare bedroom to play bass through my headphone amp. Taking musical breaks was so incredibly helpful. Nobody questioned it or even gave it much thought from what I could tell. They just accepted it. They accepted me. It was little things like this that started to make me feel human. Little by little, I didn't feel like a burden like I had my whole life. In time, I would grow to feel like as much of a gift to them as they all were to me.

It wasn't at all that I didn't like the people in her family. I still just struggled to be around anyone at that point. I got really anxious around people. Strangers in restaurants and stress were especially hard, but even at family gatherings, with a room full of people talking, I got overwhelmed quickly. Having a private room where I could retreat with my bass made all the difference in the world. I still was anxious when I returned to the family, but it was easier knowing that I had that respite when and if I needed it.

36

ONE STEP FORWARD, TWO STEPS...

Do or do not, there is no try.

Yoda

As amazing as my new life was, there were times of great difficulty and embarrassment. On New Year's Eve, we rented a cabin in the woods with vaulted ceilings, towering glass windows, and a hot tub on the deck. It even had a groovy loft bedroom for Jazmin and her friend. We cooked a delicious dinner and the girls had recently gotten out of the hot tub and were inside playing games and making TikTok videos. I had recently mentioned to the girls it was getting late and they would need to wind down soon and have quiet time. Lesli and I were out on the deck, talking and having a drink. I had already had a few beers and something was said that set me off. Lesli reacted to my comments and I took what she said horribly wrong. I threw my can at the railing and stormed inside slamming the door. The girls were alarmed and Lesli was instantly shocked and extremely upset.

The outburst brought back horrible memories of her being in a verbally abusive relationship with her children's father. She made it very clear at that moment that she would not subject her daughter to such behavior. After the initial eruption, I was embarrassed and upset with myself. I didn't want to be that kind of person. I never wanted to act that way, but I had and I was sickened by my behavior. I apologized to all three of them several times and to my surprise, each of them was understanding and accepting.

I sincerely wanted to be the most amazing parent and I knew to be given that chance again was a true gift. I struggled though, often upset with either something Jazmin was doing, or not doing, or with my behavior in relation to it. Often, I was silent, fuming just underneath the surface, trying to maintain my composure. In my mind, when she had fun with her friends, got loud in her room, or interrupted what I wanted to be doing, she was completely out of hand. I knew this was irrational, and connected to my distorted upbringing, but I couldn't help the visceral reactions that arose in me, often quite suddenly.

This underlying frustration continued to be unresolved until recently. Lesli brought to my attention that I was often very critical of Jazmin. I was not being verbally critical to her face but would make offside comments without her in the room. At first, I took this completely the wrong way. I felt as if she was comparing me to the worst person I had ever known, my mother. My mother's criticism of me was relentless and in my mind, continues to this day even though I haven't spoken to her in many years. I was pretty upset for a while, but I listened and instead of reacting, I contemplated what she had said for a short time.

In the past, I might have been unsettled for much longer, but because of all the work I had been doing, I managed to turn it around quickly. Writing this book has certainly helped with that process, too. It has facilitated my healing by allowing me a forum to express all that's in my head and helped me develop a deeper understanding of what was brewing under the surface.

I realized that Lesli was telling me this out of love and for my benefit. My entire goal in this process was to be the best version of myself in each new moment. I can't do that if I am unwilling to hear from others where I have room for improvement. I realized it doesn't have to be about what I am doing wrong, but what I could do better. I knew exactly where my behavior was coming from. That was how I was treated as a child. In my bad experience, my mother was critical and demeaning to my face. To me, both were the same and I did not want to repeat that pattern. I immediately started carefully observing every thought I had about Jazmin. I knew with conscious effort and awareness, I could improve my reaction and make things better. After only a few weeks since that late-night conversation, I was already able to notice a huge shift in my frame of reference.

I immediately took on an acute observation of my thought processes. In doing so, I realized that Jazmin, much like my own children, was somewhat estranged from her father. I can't imagine how difficult that would be. I recognized that I must, at every opportunity, choose love. When I get frustrated at dishes in the sink, I must choose love. I choose love because I know that in the grand scheme of things, it doesn't matter. What matters is that she knows completely that I am here for her. Part of rewriting the script in my head is the mantra, I choose love.

At the core of all healing lies an opportunity for expanding our perspective and enriching our thoughts. My thoughts were constantly interrupted, hijacked, or corrupted by past events and my angst over myself. From the first moment I talked to Lesli on the phone, she started recording over the dreadful tape loop that was playing in my head. In that first call, when she had me almost yelling "I AM AMAZING," it was a subtle, yet powerful seed. My whole view of myself slowly started to change. When I write about the process of growth, the reorganization of my thought patterns takes center stage. I started to paint a new landscape in my mind. Instead of jagged edges, I crafted soft, rolling hills. Instead of stagnant, murky pools, I built beautiful, clear mountain lakes. I slowly began to replace 'I can't' with maybe, and then, 'Yes, I can' ...which eventually became 'I did.' She was there to celebrate every single victory, no matter how small. I also knew that there was no such thing as failure. If I tried, then I still succeeded and was acknowledged for the effort.

I began to realize when I was confronted with criticism or confrontation, the past came roaring back and amidst the panic, I would react poorly. During that time, I would often lash out verbally or by slamming a door or something. A part of me was just trying to stop the criticism altogether, even if it was constructive advice I misinterpreted as a critique. When this happened, I would usually realize later that the person was actually trying to help me improve myself, but in my mind in that moment, I was doing everything wrong. I needed to be fixed, I was broken and 12 years old all over again. With Lesli's help and a fair amount of therapy, I began to rewrite the narrative in my mind and create new thought pathways.

I have learned in therapy when past trauma is triggered by a current event, the brain doesn't know the present from the past. For me, this meant that when Jazmin did something to upset me, I was in the throes of my mother's verbal assaults all over again. My rational brain was cast aside and I was left clinging to fight or flight.

Sometimes things happen to you that surface later and are profound all over again. When I was talking to the therapist at the group home about my mother pushing my buttons, her profound question "What are your buttons?" helped me navigate future visits with my mother because I approached every encounter with her differently. Recently, I took that same approach with my fear of being in public, being a parent, and overall relationships in my life. If I knew Jazmin had a guest coming over, I learned to approach it differently. I would view it not as an inconvenience, but as an opportunity - a chance to explore, grow, and learn about myself. In that action, I took a dramatic step away from the past, and the tape of my mother's voice that held me captive for so long. In making that choice, I love myself, and in turn, everyone involved.

It wasn't an easy hurdle to overcome. At times, the challenge still presents itself, but with practice and focus, I have been able to stay calm and utilize the rational side of my brain. The fight or flight reaction still gets me occasionally, but I am more easily and quickly able to turn it around. Choosing to develop my emotional intelligence has given me the power to react more constructively to things that may trigger me. Knowing what my buttons are and learning to understand their source helps me be responsive instead of reactive. I must remember that while I can't control anybody else's actions or words, I can control my reaction to them.

37

AND STILL, THE PAST

Happiness can only exist in acceptance.

George Orwell

So much of what everyone else takes for granted, I have struggled with tremendously. For a long time, I was triggered with intense anxiety every time somebody came to the door. From my days in my apartment where I repeatedly hallucinated that people were breaking in through my front door, I was instantly terrified when somebody knocked. This was difficult for friends and family to understand. They didn't know why they couldn't just come over and were asked to call first. To them, nobody had ever actually broken into my apartment. To me, I had too many break-ins to count. Even though some of the events that were traumatic to me were hallucinations, the trauma is completely real. My brain doesn't know the difference. To this day many years later, Lesli, Jazmin, family, bandmates, and friends all still let me know before they knock on the door.

I have also struggled immensely at times with being in public. Often, my paranoia would get the best of me. With the presence of cameras everywhere, I was constantly overcome with thoughts of who may be watching or spying on me. I was consumed with fear that the cell phones in everyone's pocket were seconds away from snapping a video. I'm still convinced they're always listening, just ask Siri.

When I met Lesli, everyone had a cell phone but me. I was too paranoid about being tracked to have one. This was a double negative for me because if I did venture out and ran into trouble, I would have no lifeline to Lesli or anyone else. At the time, I also had crushing anxiety every time I left home. It caused me a great deal of angst to go to a restaurant, even if it was only moderately busy. Jazmin was a cheerleader and I wanted so badly to be supportive and go to her games and competitions. I was completely unnerved by the amount of people, what they might be thinking, and if they would follow me home. I tried to go but spent the vast majority of the time in the car listening to music.

Once again, Lesli and I always celebrated my strength and courage just because I had tried. Each time I succeeded, even if only for a few minutes, there was a growing force of tenacity that would continue to take root in my mind. This continual celebration helped me build resilience and bravery. Over time, I was able to do things I never thought would be possible with my illness. Every victory inspired me to try something harder. Before I knew it, I was accomplishing anything I set my mind to.

I've had people say to me, 'Not everyone can do what you do.' I disagree with that statement. In 2017, I was 297 pounds and was afraid to leave my apartment. If that version of me was asked to do what I do now, I would have told you it was never going to happen. One step at a time, victory after victory, I kept moving forward. The mind can achieve the impossible. You just have to believe it can be done. I am reminded of the quote by Napoleon Hill, "Whatever the mind can conceive and believe, it can achieve." All those years ago, I started to believe. Now I know it so completely, there will never be a version of me that returns to that dark and lonely place. Don't let anyone tell you that it can't be done. Above all else, tell yourself that it can.

38

EMBRACING CHANGE

*The ache for home lives in all of us,
the safe place where we can go as we are and not be questioned.*

Maya Angelou

In the fall of 2021, Lesli took a job in Fayetteville, about an hour north. We had been discussing moving to a location that would be better for all of us. Fayetteville had better schools and a richer culture for Jazmin. It also had better opportunities for Lesli to pursue her career. For me, it housed a vibrant music scene that included much more jazz than I had access to in Ft. Smith.

A big bonus I did not anticipate from the change was extra quality time with Jazmin. With Lesli commuting, that meant time after school and dinners together, just the two of us. I really enjoyed spending that time with her and being in that role for her. I know that she liked it, too, and that felt amazing.

I did miss Lesli, but she has incredible intuition about this kind of thing. I had learned early on, to not only trust it but to dive right in. The new job was extremely demanding, so Lesli was often late getting home. I was grateful for the time with Jazmin, but my anxiety about the move was steadily building.

Selling the house meant a lot of people coming and going. Painters were working around the house. Random people would stop by to purchase things we had listed online, such as the entertainment center and the trampoline. People were inside our home - our sanctuary. After my experience with people breaking into my apartment, all the paranoia and anxiety came roaring back like a locomotive ripping through a parking lot.

I remember the first time somebody came to look at the house. Lesli's mom came over to show it since Lesli was at work. I was there but feeling very reticent and stayed mostly out of sight. I was convinced they were thinking I was completely weird. I envisioned them taking inventory of what was in the house so they could come back and rob us. I was trying not to shake visibly but my entire body was ratcheting away. I was sure that everyone saw this.

The open house was too much for me, so Lesli helped me come up with a plan. Thankfully, it was early fall and a nice day. About an hour before people were going to start showing up, I loaded up my bass in a backpack case and packed a headphone amp, some snacks, and a big water bottle. I walked a short distance from the house to a secluded park. I listened to music and played bass for several hours.

It was a constant fight to keep the intrusive thoughts of people casing our home for robbery or contemplating murder from dominating my mind and taking over. I pushed them away by playing along with Brad Mehldau. I wailed away at the most complicated tunes I could manage. Over and over, I dove deep into the complexity of the melodies and angular rhythms. It was hard for me to think about anything else while doing this. Along with always being a salve on the open wound of my anxiety, complex music was like rock climbing without a rope. It's hard to think of anything except exactly what you are doing.

The days following the open house were more difficult than the event itself. The nights were worse. I was constantly alert to every car that seemed to slow as it passed the house. I was convinced that someone would barge in at any moment, especially at night. While I never hallucinated that people were breaking in, I would wake up in the middle of the night trembling and convinced that they were coming.

On the flip side, I was encouraged by our new house. As it was being built, we took trips to see it. Our current house faced a rather busy street, so it was hard to relax with cars rumbling past all day long. We were also close to an elementary school, so there was a lot of school traffic and a fair amount of people walking by each day.

Our new house was in a new neighborhood, all the way at the back. The backyard looked out onto an open field with mountains in the distance. The best part was the living room was at the back of the house facing south. This meant no cars passing by, nobody walking by the windows, and plenty of beautiful sunshine.

Moving day finally came just several days before Christmas. In a flurry of activity, we were packed, loaded, and on our way to the new house. The whole thing went off without a hitch. Every day there has truly felt like home. I often call Lesli 'min ekta hjem' which means 'my true home' in Norwegian.

Just as I felt a beautiful sense of home in Lesli from the first day I met her, this home would soon become the foundation for new aspects of my life that, at the time, I couldn't possibly have fathomed. It would be the launch pad, not just for new activities, but a quality of life I never thought I would have. A new version of me that would rise to change not only my world but potentially the lives of thousands of other people as well.

39

UP ON THE STAGE

Without music, life would be a mistake.

Fredrich Nietzsche

Living in a constant state of anxiety impedes your quality of life. I existed in that world, and it affected my role in the family, but also my ability to perform as a musician. I had been playing bass in a room by myself for six and a half years. I had performed almost daily for Lesli but was far too anxious and self-conscious to play in public. She consistently encouraged me and told me how talented I was. Slowly, I started to think about performing in public in front of strangers...strangers with cameras. I had been doing some research about the local music scene and knew there were a couple of open mics in town. I finally worked up the courage and decided to give it a shot. Above all, I knew that Lesli would celebrate with me regardless of whether or not I succeeded. The true victory was in making the attempt itself. Even if I didn't play, she would celebrate that I left the house and showed up.

Eventually, the night came and I was exceedingly anxious and overthinking everything. There was an open mic at a local place called Six Twelve Coffeehouse & Bar. It was only two miles from our house and had great reviews. I was nervous so I drank a few beers before we left. We arrived at the venue a little early. It was a quaint little bar with local artists' paintings and photographs displayed. It had a very welcoming ambiance, lit softly and with a modern slant on the furniture and tables. There were several groups of people talking and a couple of tables with individuals using a laptop and wearing headphones. I had called ahead of time and spoken to the guy who organized the event. His name was Riley. He had let me know they had a PA system, so all I had to bring was myself and my bass. We walked in and I was feeling determined, but the anxiety was still growing inside. I saw a man with a clipboard or small chalkboard standing near the makeshift stage. I walked over to him and introduced myself. This was the first time I met Riley. He offered a warm welcome with kindness in his eyes and a pure heart. He seemed a little surprised when I said I was playing bass by myself, but quickly signed me up. His smile was very encouraging.

The worst part was the waiting. I learned quickly that open mic night was one of the most popular nights at Six Twelve. I had to wait for my turn to play and I almost bailed a million times. I had another beer while I was waiting. One of the daunting things for me about open mics was that you are not only going up in front of strangers, but a good portion of them are musicians. It's kind of like reading your book in front of a room full of writers.

When it was finally my turn, I set up quickly with trembling hands. I felt as if I would collapse at any moment. As soon as I hit that first note, my anxiety immediately melted away. I was in my safe place again. The world disappeared and I played. I opened with Giant Steps by John Coltrane, then followed with Giggles - a song I wrote for my wife. Even in front of all those strangers, it was just me and the music. It was the first monumental step into this new realm for me that would continue to grow and expand. Lesli was there for every step along the way. I didn't know it at the time, but Riley would soon become an amazing friend and confidant. He and Angie, the owner of Six Twelve, would be an integral part of my budding confidence.

After my solo performance, I reveled in my victory. My anxiety quickly returned now that I wasn't playing but was overshadowed by my feelings of triumph and achievement. The stream of musicians that were coming up to me saying that I had done a great job was an incredible distraction and made me feel on top of the world.

Riley was especially impressed and asked me to play with him for a few tunes. In short order, I was back up on stage and having the time of my life playing with him. When he was finished, the next performer wanted me to stay and play with him, too. Finally, all my years of practice, hours each day, were paying off. I was able to pick up what they were doing quickly and add creative elements and countermelodies even though we had never played together before.

Music is not only a language; it is perhaps the most unique language that humans have ever known. Music not only allows for individual creativity and expression, but it is universal. Similar to mathematics, but with music, no matter what language you speak, I can communicate with you how I am *feeling* and you can play along. In that respect, music is distinct. The magical language of music has spoken to me in different ways throughout my life. I owe a great deal of gratitude to my high school band director. He went above and beyond to make music fun, challenging, and cool. He expanded our knowledge and taught us much more than just fundamentals. We learned about modes and polyrhythms. More importantly, we learned that music was more than a hobby, it was a lifetime of joy and for me, salvation.

Playing at the open mic was truly an amazing experience. I wanted to stay up all night and start working on music for the next one. My childlike wonder for music had returned. In this first venture back out into the world of music, I was reminded of the story and struggles of Jaco Pastorius. He was incredible in his virtuosity, but equally disheveled in his ability to perform ordinary tasks. He got more and more unpredictable and disruptive until his violent death at an early age. His music has always inspired me. His creativity is unparalleled, and he redefined what a person could do with the bass guitar. Up until that point, no bassist had ever played or written music the way that he did. No musician can play bass now and not stand on his shoulders to some degree. He will always be an inspiration but is also a reminder of how things can go awry when your mental health is not given priority.

Bolstered by the feedback from that evening, I started going regularly to the open mic at Six Twelve. At this point, I still needed liquid courage to help me. I always drank before and throughout the evening to get myself to a place where I felt brave enough to get up on stage. The good part about the open mic was that I could bail without disappointing anyone. In other words, no other band members were counting on me. The hard part was waiting for my turn. Riley was a wonderful friend right from the beginning. He was always trying to get me on the list in whatever spot in the lineup I wanted to be. Usually, this was right away. I knew that, if I could just stay long enough to get on stage, the world would fall away with that first note.

For about a year, I continued to go to open mics and always had a few drinks before and during the show. One night, Riley was ill and asked if I would be willing to set up and host the open mic. My day had been wrought with symptoms and I was still having murmurs off and on. I wanted to be helpful, so I reluctantly agreed.

Jazmin had cheer practice that night, so Lesli had prior commitments and couldn't join me until much later in the evening. I don't recall drinking heavily that night, but I must have been placating my anxiety more than usual. By the time Lesli arrived, I was quite inebriated and it showed. Lesli smiled and said nothing at the time, but later told me about how people were rolling their eyes and shaking their heads. Before I knew it, I had become that guy. I didn't play well either when I drank. By this time, I had graduated to playing more and more complicated tunes, like Portrait of Tracy by Jaco, and I couldn't play them with the articulation they demanded while under the influence of alcohol.

We were sitting at dinner the next night when she gently brought up the subject and shared her observation. It all came full circle as the words fell on me like a gentle afternoon light. I had been in this place before, with someone telling me how to be a better version of myself, but this was the first time that I didn't get defensive, take it personally, or pull away. She was the light in my garden after the rain. I sat there across from her, so grateful for her and her love. I knew in that moment, that I could do anything I set my heart and mind to, and that I could do it without alcohol. I knew that I would be a better parent, a better husband, and a better musician. I made a pact with myself that night to always perform sober and decided I would reserve social drinking for special occasions with just Lesli and me.

I held to my agreement with myself. I felt better and could think more clearly. I was less prone to outbursts, and I played better. As Riley and my friend Eli said, open mics became "The Todd Show." I was up there most of the night, playing with various other musicians. Eventually, I started to think that maybe I could do a show by myself. I felt like it would not only be entertaining but also a great goal for me to set as the next challenge for myself.

I approached Angie, the owner, and she agreed that we should give it a shot. She checked the schedule and I was suddenly slated for a spot to have my debut. I was quite anxious in the two weeks leading up to the show. I practiced more than ever, worried I would forget, screw up, or the audience would hate it. Lesli kept encouraging me and that was all I needed.

The night of the show there were a fair number of people there, mostly strangers, but a few friends, including Riley and Eli. Most importantly, Lesli was there, front and center. Once again, when I hit that first note, the world disappeared. For two hours, I was in my element, just me and my bass. The performance went really well. I played a 50/50 mix of my original solo bass songs, and the rest were me playing along with songs on my iPod.

Over the next few months, I eventually shifted to solo shows that were almost 100% original material. I would occasionally play covers, such as 'So What' by Miles Davis, but I would design my own arrangement where I played or created all the parts. I was also invited to play at other venues, including a winery. I was constantly practicing and composing new songs. I got better and better at creating different soundscapes with my bass. Eventually, I added piano, which brought an interesting wrinkle into each performance. Angie was so impressed with my creativity and all the positive feedback she got from customers and her staff, that she offered me a regular spot every month for the upcoming year. She said, "To both draw a crowd and engage an audience with simply bass and piano is really incredible!!"

I became the only solo bass and piano show in town. My shows ranged from ambient to funk, then back to jazz and classical. I worked hard to not only entertain but do so in a way that nobody could walk away without at least a little wonder. My confidence as a musician was soaring and my joy as a parent and husband grew with every new moment.

Each time I played I met more musicians interested in what I was doing. I had several offers to join bands, including one from my friend, Riley, but I turned them all down. I desperately wanted the joy of playing with other people, but the wall of protection I had constructed in my mind was too tall. I saw it as a shield for myself and for them. I believed if I joined a band, I was only setting everyone up for disappointment. There had already been several open mics I had planned to attend, but voices or anxiety entrapped me once again on those days. I stayed home instead.

If I was in a band, people would be counting on me. If we had a gig, and I woke up with voices that day, I would have to find a sub at the last minute, or they would have to do without my contribution. I didn't want to do that. I didn't want to let anyone down. There was still the constant voice from my childhood playing in my head that made me feel like I was about to do something wrong at any moment, so I avoided being in a position of potential failure at all costs.

Lesli and I rarely had conversations about my medication, unless it was her doing the quick double check each week when I filled my pill box. Around this time, Lesli suggested that I talk to my doctor about possibly lowering the dose of my mood stabilizer. We had discussed the fact that this particular medication was a prime culprit for causing my social anxiety. It was prescribed to help minimize my mania symptoms and I had shown no signs of those for quite some time, so it was working well for that purpose. During the next appointment with my psychiatrist, I talked to her about the reduction and she agreed to try it.

I felt better almost immediately. Just the slight reduction reduced my anxiety, made me more animated, and gave me more energy throughout the day. I was careful to monitor how often I struggled with sleeping through the night, as that was the first sign that my mania was returning, and my dose was too low.

It's important to take your meds as prescribed. If your quality of life is not the best that it can be, work with your doctor to improve it. Never settle. Lesli taught me that. It's so important to find a great doctor and have a partner to monitor you and let you know how you are doing with whatever medications you are on. I also keep a journal that chronicles my symptoms. This is valuable when I have my appointments with my doctor because I can look at and specifically tell her when I had symptoms and what happened.

My confidence continued to grow and I eventually formed a jazz trio. I not only played bass but also contacted potential venues and booked shows. This was a huge step forward for me. A year earlier, because of paranoia, I didn't even have a cell phone. Now, I not only had one, but I was cold-calling strangers and coordinating events with the band. I flourished in this role. I was the most prepared member, and ironically enough, was the most dependable. While others would flake at rehearsal or schedule a sub for a show, I was always there, right where I said I would be, voices or not. Lesli still reminds me how I went from being terrified to show up at an open mic to being a band manager in a jazz trio, to playing three-hour solo shows in a short period of only two years.

With my success, I finally mustered up the courage to make it through an entire cheer competition. I truly enjoyed being there for Jazmin. For a long time, I agonized over what to say when other parents would inevitably ask, "So what do you do?" I could say I'm on disability, but sometimes they want to know why. I could lie and say I'm retired, but I don't look *that* old. Amid all the internal turmoil and mental frustration that accompanies any great effort to overcome the past, I was finally feeling confident. I am overjoyed to say that during the success of this musical journey, I started to say simply, "I'm a musician."

40

PUSHING THROUGH

Man is not made for defeat.
A man can be destroyed but not defeated.

Earnest Hemingway

    If there is one thing that my mother gave me that I am grateful for, it is my all-consuming drive to never fail. I was told repeatedly that I would, so from an early age I relentlessly pursued whatever was in front of me. It's not that I didn't fail, and when I did, I took it all that much harder. It did, however, create in me an unwavering work ethic that has helped me succeed. Initially, it was school and college that motivated me. The thought of getting away from home drove me to study like a maniac. It eventually translated into running, music, and more recently, self-improvement. I trained intensely and consistently until I ran an ultra-marathon. I practiced non-stop for hours on end until I was able to do a three-hour solo show and release several albums. At every turn, I pushed myself to practice, to process, and to train until it was almost impossible for me to fail.

    About 18 months ago, Lesli suggested I learn Portrait of Tracy by Jaco Pastorius. She remembered me saying when we first met that I wanted to learn that song someday. I rebuffed her at first, saying something about how hard it was, but the seed had been planted. At first, it seemed unimaginable, but that only made me try harder. That refusal to fail was ignited, and within two weeks, I was playing it fluently. Now, it's my warmup tune. Was it obsession? Maybe. Overall, I think it's been a healthy one for me because I have used it to overcome what seemed like insurmountable goals. With each new victory, my self-worth was strengthened, and my self-doubt diminished. Baby steps are still steps and ones that can lead you across mountains, whether they are in the wilderness or the far reaches of your mind.

I also found a new passion of focus – self-improvement. Opening up to Lesli and my therapist completely helped me gain an unwavering sense of belonging. I used to always feel alone. I wasn't living in the forest or trekking through the desert, but my isolation and fear made me feel like I was. Taking a constant inventory of my words and actions and reminding myself of what I can do better next time have kept me grounded and engaged.

Over the last few years, I have gone from taking everything personally and being deeply affected by all that surrounds me, to being able to let go, sit back, and observe. As Lao Tzu wrote, "The world is won by those who let it go." I am not just noticing what everyone else is doing, but I am actively discerning my thoughts, actions, and feelings. I started by tuning in to everything that was going on inside of me. The deeper I looked, the deeper I wanted to go. It has been a very positive cycle.

Writing this book has been a very cathartic and empowering process. At times it was very difficult. Writing about my childhood or failures as a father was excruciating. There were many days and weeks I could only write for ten minutes before I had to play bass for an hour to clear my head. I had terrible nightmares, as writing jarred loose elements of my past that I had placed away and not considered for a long time.

In the end, I know myself better now than I ever have. The value of self-knowledge cannot be bought online or purchased in a bookstore, but the benefits of that exploration are priceless. The level of self-awareness I now carry with me affords me the ability to publish my darkest moments. Climbing out from beneath the ice to face my worst demons was agonizing. After all the paranoia and psychosis I endured, allowing my secrets to be 'out there' is a monumental accomplishment. My anxiety builds from time to time at the thought of publishing them to the world and I feel afraid. On the other side of fear, I know to help as many people as possible I must be more courageous than I have ever been.

41

POWER RUN

*Only those who will risk going too far
can possibly find out how far one can go.*

T.S. Eliot

As I was growing more comfortable with music shows and being in public, I decided to start running again. When I was running in my early 20s, my purpose was to isolate myself from everyone else. I spent my whole life around someone who constantly berated and doubted me, so I became withdrawn and craved seclusion. I was unaware of this pattern at the time, so I didn't realize my running obsession was causing me to miss out on copious amounts of valuable family time. I sometimes think I lost as much time with them because I was running as I did when I was in the throes of schizophrenia.

My motivation to run now has drastically changed. I am no longer running away from my problems or trauma. I am moving toward and through them, with eyes wide open and definiteness of purpose. I have realized it's important not only to feel strong but to know you are strong. Whether it's physical or mental, running helps foster the creation of a core belief deep within.

The inner knowing that, "I AM AMAZING!"

I am a survivor and my mental illness does not define me - I DO.

One day last spring, I went out for a run. Within a minute of leaving the driveway, Fred showed up in his checkered suit. He was running around yelling and ringing people's doorbells. I was completely convinced someone was going to open their door to see what was happening and call the police. After a short time, I realized he was a hallucination, but my mind was telling me he was real. As I mentioned before, hallucinations are kind of like having a dream. While you are inside the dream, you accept what you see as fact, no matter how bizarre it may be. Eventually my rational brain returns, but it takes a while.

For the first time in my life, something in me shifted and I decided to fight back. Up until this point, I would have booked it home and isolated myself until he went away. That day, I kept running. I ran for over twenty minutes with him careening around. Shortly before I got home, he was gone. It showed me I was stronger than this disease. I had within me the power to not only fight back but to WIN.

Suddenly, there was a belief in me that anything was truly possible. It was the beginning of a personal best every single day. On that day running with Fred, my true path as a warrior began. It was the true catalyst for me. The switch in my mind had been flipped from 'NO' to 'GO'. One stride at a time, no matter how bad the storm, I ran through. I always knew that everything was in my mind, my hijacked brain taking control. Now, I understood that I had power over that. At any moment, I could decide to keep going. I realized during that run that I was stronger than I ever believed possible. I was certain that if I could go running outside with that hallucination, I could do anything.

Within a month, I was in a band. I had avoided this for a long time because of my schizophrenia. Running with Fred that day, I suddenly believed I could do anything.

I am reminded of the story of the four-minute mile. Doctors declared it was humanly impossible. It was a mark that athletes tried to reach for decades. Then it was broken. Within ten years, 24 other people broke that barrier. Nothing changed. They simply *knew* it could be done. That belief paved the way to their success.

By this time, I had been to the local jazz jam a few times and had met some musicians in the area. With my passion for jazz, I reached out to a jazz piano player I knew and he was open to jam. Soon, we found a good drummer and scheduled our first practice. Our jazz trio, Flat Five, quickly built up a setlist and was ready to start booking shows. I was the bandleader, so I took on the responsibility of calling venues and working with them to get our band in the door. This was huge for me, as talking on the phone with anyone has always been difficult. Now, I was talking to strangers almost daily.

Our first few shows went well. One day, we were scheduled to play a Sunday brunch at a new venue. I had practiced the set list many times and was excited to perform. The show was outside on the patio and the weather was beautiful. I woke up that morning with voices. I knew canceling or finding a sub was out of the question. It was essential for me to be there. It was a new venue and I was the point of contact. More importantly, jazz is too complicated for someone to fill in at the last minute. Aside from the complexity, there are many nuances of group and individual improvisation that take time to develop as a band. In a jazz trio, the bass is a critical component. It is the anchor for rhythm and harmony. Without it, you lose a key element of the band.

I remembered my run with Fred. I loaded up the car and put my headphones on for the hour-long drive to the show. While we were setting up, I almost told my bandmates about my symptoms several times but decided to keep what was going on to myself. The voice I was hearing that day was Fred. He didn't appear visually but was rambling on in a monotone voice about how to replace the drum brakes on a tractor-trailer. It was very difficult to concentrate. By the end of the show, I was mentally exhausted from having to pay attention to the music while hearing his voice in my head the whole time. But I did it. I fought, and I won, all over again.

At the end of the second set, I finally told the drummer what was going on. He was blown away. He knew I had schizophrenia but said if I hadn't told him he never would have realized what was happening. My playing was flawless despite the struggle I was wrestling. Lesli was proud of me, too. I felt victorious. All I ever wanted to do was to be able to do what normal people do. I realized then that I was doing *more* than what normal people do. I was battling voices and playing jazz in front of strangers. Suddenly the impossible felt within my grasp.

As the band continued to book gigs, I was elated to be playing jazz and doing what I loved. I was also running. When I began, I started running every other day. I felt so great on my running days, that Lesli suggested that I run more often. I now run six days a week, no matter what my mental health is putting me through. Every time I have symptoms, I run. If they are not completely gone when I am finished, they are severely diminished.

The routine of my daily run is very important to me. I don't always run at the same time every day, but it's usually in the morning. I especially enjoy the early hours well before dawn. The streets are serene and pious. The world becomes my church as my foot strikes the steady thrum of a sermon soothing my soul.

It took me many years to realize it, but I know now that my mental health comes first. It is more important than anyone or anything. My life is a testament to the fact that mental health is a life-and-death matter. Running is my daily sojourn to cleanse my soul and settle my mind. When you take a trip in an airplane, one of the first things they tell you is to put your oxygen mask on first. The reason for this is simple. You can't help anyone else if you are dead. Running is one of my oxygen masks. Along with music and medication, it creates a foundation for me to have the best quality of life and be helpful to others.

Running has taught me how important it is to continue through the uncomfortable moments. I do that not just physically, but mentally. Even on a good day, with my schizophrenia, I never know what may be lurking around the next corner during every single run. I try not to think about it, but in a way, good days are harder than those with symptoms. At least when I have symptoms, the voices or hallucinations are a constant that I can accept and fight against. When nothing is going on, the possibility that something might suddenly happen or someone might come from behind the next house and run after me is very real. I guess nobody ever really knows what is going to happen to them out there, but my mental illness creates an uncertainty that makes even the most casual run daunting.

This past weekend, I awoke to Fred jumping around and pacing at the end of the bed in the dark. It was 4 a.m. It took a few terrifying moments for my rational brain to kick in and realize that he was a hallucination. Once I did, I got dressed and headed out for a run. I only lasted five minutes. He was running around setting off car alarms and breaking windows. In front of me was a quiet street, hopeful and full of solace. Behind me was a path of chaos and destruction at the hands of Fred. Even though I knew he was a hallucination, I was certain an angry neighbor or cop was going to chase me down at any moment. It's hard to deny reality when you're experiencing it.

I came home and played my bass with headphones for an hour and a half. He was in there with me but was quietly playing cards in the corner. One of the hardest things about schizophrenia is the feeling that you are never truly alone. Even when you are, someone like Fred could show up at any moment. I always have a constant noise floor of anxiety.

Lesli reminded me recently that it's important for me to acknowledge how much I fight these battles on my own. Sure, her support and encouragement are amazing, but in the end, I'm the one 'in the arena' as Teddy Roosevelt said. No one was there in the dark, urging me out the door. Lesli was asleep. It was just me and I knew what I needed to do.

No one was there, for all my years in the wilderness, or for years when I lived on my own. I've made great strides towards an amazing quality of life in the last few years and Lesli has certainly been an integral part of that journey. However, at the end of each day, I'm the one who carries the sword. It's almost as if I was driving a boat through a quagmire of rocky outcroppings and dangerous reefs. She puts out buoys, warning me of where not to go, but in the end, I am the one driving the boat.

I can still crash; I can still decide. I can shut off the engine and not make any progress or I can keep going. It's up to me.

    Later that same day, Lesli encouraged me to try again. It was around noon and Fred was still hanging out, peeking out from around corners and pacing here and there. I laced up and hit the road. As I ran, he was running with me. My heart was pounding and my stride was swift and purposeful. My goal was to run fast enough to get rid of him. After about a mile, he veered off into the neighborhood and that was the last I saw of him.

    I stayed out there and ran for five miles that day, just to make sure he was gone. I was proud of myself for being brave and trying again. It took all the courage I had to go out again after the car alarm ordeal. But I did. I ran and I won. Lesli tells me all the time I have earned every drop of ink in the warrior rune tattoo on my hand. I believe in myself more with every step. Strength can be encouraged, but in the end, it comes from within. So many times in the past, I would have given up and suffered with symptoms for the entire day. On that day, I chose to fight.

    As I continue to take the next step in my healing, there are always opportunities that arise to challenge my commitment and resolve. Even though I have come a long way, I am still not free from my triggers and traumas. Recently, Jazmin was off from school for the holidays and had a friend staying with her. The first day and night passed without too much trouble since they were not home very much. The second day, it was raining all day, so we were all at the house together.

    They were really good and had been mostly quiet and considerate. Occasionally, there would be a sudden loud burst of laughter, then silence again. Next, a door would shut, then quiet. Then, a round of animated conversation would echo down the hallway. Throughout the day, I was feeling agitated and uneasy. It took me a while to realize what was bothering me so much. When I was in my apartment, I was constantly enduring random loud noises. This was a whole day of that. By the end of the day, I was frazzled and exhausted but I was grateful I made it through the day without an outburst. This was certainly an accomplishment over past experiences. As I said before, baby steps are still steps.

42

ABOVE IT ALL

Man cannot discover new oceans unless he has the courage to lose sight of the shore.

Andre Gide

One day last summer, I came across an article announcing a newly scheduled performance for the Brad Mehldau Trio in Milwaukee. The show was in November a few days before my birthday. I never dreamed I would end up in the front row just a few short months later. When my wife came home that evening, I told her about the concert. Without hesitation, she grabbed her computer and started searching. Within minutes, she had tickets bought, an airline ticket secured, and hotel reservations made. Never once did she doubt that I could make the trip. I sat in the kitchen in complete awe that I was going to see Brad. I was so excited. I never dreamed I would end up in the front row just a few short months later.

I hadn't been on a plane in decades. The thought of cameras and security guards was too much for me to endure. With my confidence continuing to grow, I was determined to do it – by myself. This was a monumental step forward and a resounding victory on all fronts. I went there not only to see Brad Mehldau in concert, but to visit the church where I had been found as a baby, and most importantly, to prove to myself that I could.

It's not just important to *think* you are strong. It's important to prove that you are. This trip was my statement to the world and myself that;

I am strong.

As I looked out the plane window, I suddenly felt as if I had been asleep my whole life; surviving inside a dream where my days turned into nightmares from which I was unable to awaken. Now, the events of the last few years lit up in my mind like the lights on the ground as we approached the city of my birth. They lit my path like hyphens between my dreams. I grew more and more aware of myself in this existence, this time, and when the thud of the wheels touching down shuddered through the cabin, I was awake. For the first time, I was strong in my core and witnessed everything around me with the knowledge that whatever the world had in store for me, I would be ready. I would be alright.

Walking through the airport, my feet weren't hitting the ground. I was feeling so alive and exhilarated. It was late at night around 10 and even though I had to find a way to my hotel, I had full confidence I was on the right path. I found a cab immediately. During the ride, I remembered how only a few short years ago I agonized over my short rides to the doctor and therapist. I was anxious for days before and after the appointments. I was a complete wreck by the time I got home. Now, I was cruising the streets with a stranger, window slightly open, chatting off and on, and enjoying the vistas of the big city.

I checked in to the hotel, opened the door to my room, dropped my bag, and stood at the twenty-foot window with a lifetime of struggle having finally been lifted off my shoulders. I had endured 26 years of schizophrenia. The madness and chaos it brings to everyday life are impossible to understand unless you have lived it. In that moment, I knew it would always be with me, lurking around any corner, but now I was finally strong enough to weather any storm it could muster. The love of my wife and family, along with my own determination and courage, had finally set me free.

I survived a childhood of verbal and emotional abuse and neglect. The weight of this burden carried on into my adulthood as I learned to cope with the constant fight or flight response to everyday events that triggered my trauma. I was never given the necessary tools to navigate the ebb and flow of life. No one instilled the knowledge of how to handle the ups and downs that certainly come. Despite all of this, I never used it as an excuse for bad behavior. I never played the victim. I ended the cycle of trauma and was now standing in the city of my birth with the world laid out before me like a blank canvas vibrating with endless possibilities.

As the night was growing longer, I knew it was time to get some rest. The large windows were somewhat majestic, but the room was cavernous and eerily quiet. I was away from my comfort zone and had trouble falling asleep. I didn't have the familiarity of my amazing wife lying next to me. I missed her breathing and subtle shifting as I drifted off to sleep. I wanted so badly to be close to her and kiss her once more, as I do every night before we fell asleep. Eventually, the long day of travel combined with my night meds caught up with me and I fell asleep. Not deeply, but asleep. I woke up at about 3:30 a.m., and for a few seconds didn't remember where I was. I checked the weather, dressed, stretched, and went for my first run in Wisconsin in over 20 years.

The city was quiet and I could feel the first breaths of winter upon my face. My steps carried me down to the river and along the trail. I had to consciously force myself not to run at a blistering pace. I was so excited to be here; I was so proud to have made it. It was a great first view of the sleeping urban landscape. The dark water of the river reflected the lights of the city. The air was crisp and clean with the slightest scent of exhaust. Step by step, I carried myself past the shoulders of the proud buildings in the historical district. Freedom is running when nothing is chasing you. On that run, I was truly free.

When I returned to the hotel, I showered and went down to breakfast. It had been several months since the medication change that helped reduce my social anxiety, but after so many years of living with it, I was still caught off guard by the absence of it. It's kind of like the first warm day after a long cold winter; you're still expecting it to be cold when you walk outside. There was a fair amount of people in the dining area, including a table of men from Denmark. I recognized some of their words and said hello in Norwegian. My broken language was met with a few friendly smiles. I found an empty table and sat down and enjoyed my meal. After decades of never being able to enjoy anything but the rare fleeting moment at a public meal, this type of freedom was very powerful and deeply refreshing.

After breakfast, I set out to visit the church where I was abandoned as an infant. It was a short, pleasant walk from the hotel, and I found it without too much trouble. The old church was modest in size, but reverent in character. I stood at the very back, realizing it had probably not changed much in the last 51 years. The stained-glass windows towered overhead as the light slowly filtered in through the elaborate patterns. The ornate backdrop to the altar stood 40 feet or more and the whole place had a familiar and unfiltered scent, like the tweed of your grandfather's suit jacket.

I made my way to the location where the kind priest found me as a baby. It was the second pew from the back on the right side. After years of being on a heavy dose of mood stabilizers and being unable to experience my feelings, the sudden rush of emotions was a little unsettling. It had only been a few months since my med reduction and I was still getting used to it. It was so quiet I could hear my blood flowing. As I sat there, my life came flooding back to me, pieces of where I had been, when I had fallen in love, and when I had almost died. The memories were pouring into my mind, skipping from one vista to another like a fast train passing endless billboards.

I marveled at all that had happened and wondered how much would transpire before I sat in that place again. As was happening more and more frequently, my thoughts turned to possibilities and positive outcomes. My train of thought was no longer plagued with visions of doom and negativity. I was rewriting the script of my life as I dreamed of the future. It had been three and a half years since I met Lesli; since my journey had turned inward and I began fighting back. I never thought I would travel to this city alone, yet there I was. I knew that no matter how hard I tried I could not imagine where I might be in another three and a half years. I caught glimpses of me traveling around to promote this book. I could see myself speaking to mental health professionals and patients. I knew anything was possible now. I knew that my passion was to help others. I embraced this new life of freedom from the chains of my mind and knew I was never going back.

After I visited the church, I enjoyed the fresh brisk air on my way back to the hotel. The sky was bright and gentle winds seemed to cleanse my spirit. A little while later my friend Craig arrived. He was visiting from Madison and was planning to spend the day and go to the concert with me. We talked for a while about music and my trip. He commented about how much weight I had lost and noted that I seemed much less anxious. The last time I had seen him I was close to 300 pounds, and my eyes darted around constantly. Even the smallest human interaction would send me off the rails mentally and emotionally. I was now 180 pounds, and mostly anxiety free. I felt a little nervous about the concert and being in a strange city, but I think it was the normal uneasiness anyone would have. Not the 'cut your brain to ribbons with a million intrusive thoughts' kind of anxiety.

We hung out as old friends do, 'remember this...did I tell you about that'...and spent the day catching up. We are both bass players, so he brought a couple of bass guitars with him. We played off and on for a while. It was good to visit with him and it helped take my mind off my subtly growing anxiety about the concert.

After playing together and some relaxation, we went out to a nice dinner and walked to the show. We had front-row seats. I had never had tickets like this for anything in my life. My anxiety had all but disappeared as I took in the majesty of the old theater, the instruments, and the fact that I was about to see my musical hero. I was near tears when he came out with his trio and remained that way for the duration of the show. I was caught up in every note. Every movement of his hands nudged my mind a little closer to complete bliss.

He talked a bit between a few of the songs and looked directly at me a couple of times. Towards the end of the concert, he glanced over at me as he took a little bow with his hand over his heart. Several months prior, I had sent an email to his agent, detailing how his music had pulled me from the depths of suicide, and where I would be sitting at the show. I must believe in that moment; he knew it was me. They closed with a waltz and left the stage. My breath finally returned, and I stood and clapped. It didn't take long for them to return for an encore.

All those years ago, in the throes of schizophrenia and contemplating suicide, Brad was there. Playing along with him helped heal the deepest of wounds. There were other artists, but he was always my go-to. Not just in the darkness, but in the joy and light, too. Brad plays with a complexity that can be daunting even to seasoned veteran musicians. As a beginning bass player, his version of Hey Joe was one that I could not only play along with but lose myself in. It remains in my playlist titled *Clear the Mechanism* to this very day.

As they re-entered the stage for the encore, I watched as Brad sat down at the beautiful grand piano under the glowing lights and began playing. I was completely blown away. They played that very song - the song that had carried me through the demons of my mind and brought me to the light of another day that I thought I might never see. That song, as it rang out gloriously on the platform in front of me, was an anthem to my victory.

I wept.

Joy resounded in my heart in a way that music had never done before. I was overcome with the feeling that I had made it. After 51 years, perhaps to the day, I had arrived at a place where I was whole. The dreaded feeling of being broken or memories of being lost and afraid had vanished like a teardrop in the ocean. I was ME and that was enough.

When it was over, I could barely stand. As I wiped away my tears, Brad looked at me again. As I left the theater, I had no fear. No thoughts of Fred, Claire, Drake, or my mother. Just the sound of a piano. Suddenly I was four years old all over again, sitting and playing with my Bill Evans record. I knew in that moment that all I ever had was right now. I may play different notes at different times, but the only ones that truly exist are the ones that are currently sounding.

Thank you for listening. This is my song.